The Han-Xiongnu War, 133 BC–89 AD

It is sometimes said that things first come to life in the east and reach their fulfilment in the west. The beginning of an undertaking invariably occurs in the southeast, and the reaping of rewards always takes place in the northwest.
Sima Qian, Records of the Grand Historian
(translation by Burton Watson)

Ever since losing the Qilian Mountains, our herds no longer grow.
Ever since losing the Yanzhi Mountains, our women lack rouge to pretty their cheeks.
Xiongnu song

The empire, long divided, must unite; long united, must divide. Thus it has ever been.
Luo Guangzhong, Three Kingdoms
(translation by Moss Roberts)

The Han-Xiongnu War, 133 BC–89 AD

The Struggle of China and a Steppe Empire Told Through Its Key Figures

Scott Forbes Crawford

Pen & Sword
MILITARY

First published in Great Britain in 2023 by
Pen & Sword Military
An imprint of Pen & Sword Books Limited
Yorkshire – Philadelphia

Text Copyright © Scott Forbes Crawford 2023
Map Copyright © Tina Ross 2023 (www.tinaross@me.com)

ISBN 978 1 52679 066 8

The right of Scott Forbes Crawford to be identified as
Author of this Work has been asserted by him in accordance
with the Copyright, Designs and Patents Act 1988.

A CIP catalogue record for this book is
available from the British Library

All rights reserved. No part of this book may be reproduced or
transmitted in any form or by any means, electronic or mechanical
including photocopying, recording or by any information storage and
retrieval system, without permission from the Publisher in writing.

Typeset by Mac Style
Printed in the UK by CPI Group (UK) Ltd, Croydon, CR0 4YY.

Pen & Sword Books Limited incorporates the imprints of After
the Battle, Atlas, Archaeology, Aviation, Discovery, Family History,
Fiction, History, Maritime, Military, Military Classics, Politics,
Select, Transport, True Crime, Air World, Frontline Publishing, Leo
Cooper, Remember When, Seaforth Publishing, The Praetorian Press,
Wharncliffe Local History, Wharncliffe Transport, Wharncliffe True
Crime and White Owl.

For a complete list of Pen & Sword titles please contact

PEN & SWORD BOOKS LIMITED
47 Church Street, Barnsley, South Yorkshire, S70 2AS, England
E-mail: enquiries@pen-and-sword.co.uk
Website: www.pen-and-sword.co.uk
or
PEN AND SWORD BOOKS
1950 Lawrence Rd, Havertown, PA 19083, USA
E-mail: Uspen-and-sword@casematepublishers.com
Website: www.penandswordbooks.com

Contents

Chronology of Major Events in the Han-Xiongnu War   vii
Prologue: A Misread Prophecy   xii

Part One: Architects of War and Empire   1

Chapter I	Chanyu Modun (d. 174 BC): First Emperor of the Steppe	3
Chapter II	Liu Bang (256–195 BC): From Rebel to Emperor	13
Chapter III	Emperor Wu of Han (156–87 BC): The 'Martial Emperor'	21

Part Two: Steppe Soldiers   37

Chapter IV	Li Guang (d. 119 BC): The Bold and Blundering Bowman	39
Chapter V	Chanyu Yizhixie (d. 114 BC): Leader of an Embattled Empire	52
Chapter VI	Wei Qing (d. 105 BC): Strategist of the Battlefield and Court	65
Chapter VII	Huo Qubing (140–117 BC): Horseman with the Strength of the Steppe	73

Part Three: Pathfinders to the West   81

Chapter VIII	Zhang Qian (died c. 114 BC): Pioneer of the Silk Road	83
Chapter IX	Princess Jieyou (d. 49 BC): Peace Bride and Han Operative	94
Chapter X	Li Guangli (d. 88 BC): Hunter of Heavenly Horses	101

| Chapter XI | The *Chanyus* Zhizhi (d. 36 BC) and Huhanye (d. 31 BC): A Broken Brotherhood | 114 |

Part Four: Warriors at the Imperial Sunset   123

| Chapter XII | King Xian of Yarkand (d. circa AD 62): Han Ally Gone Rogue | 125 |

| Chapter XIII | Ban Chao (AD 32–102): Wielder of Brush and Sword | 133 |

| Chapter XIV | Dou Xian (d. AD 92): Final Cog in the Han War Machine | 144 |

Epilogue: Reared in Each Other's Shadows   150
Notes   153
Bibliography   158
Index   160

Chronology of Major Events in the Han-Xiongnu War

Historical figures who are subjects of their own chapters appear in bold.

221 BC – The Qin dynasty establishes the first imperial Chinese government, uniting all kingdoms under its rule.

215 BC – Qin army invades the Hexi Corridor of the Ordos Plateau, sending the Xiongnu in retreat to the northeast.

210 BC – Qin emperor Shi Huangdi dies, touching off a rebellion.

209 BC – **Modun** slays his father the *chanyu* Touman, becoming leader of the Xiongnu.

208 BC – The Qin dynasty falls.

206 BC – Outbreak of the Chu-Han Contention, in which two Chinese states vie for the imperial throne.

202 BC – **Liu Bang** prevails in the Chu-Han Contention and becomes the first emperor of the Han dynasty.

201 BC – The Xiongnu reclaim the Hexi Corridor.

200 BC – Battle of Baideng, the first major Han-Xiongnu clash.

198 BC – The Han makes its first marriage-alliance payment, securing decades of strained peace.

195 BC – Liu Bang dies from a wound sustained in a battle quelling rebellion.

C. 177 BC – The Xiongnu drive off their foe the Yuezhi and project power into the Tarim Basin.

C. 174 BC – The *chanyu* **Modun** dies.

174 BC – Chinese eunuch Zhonghang Yue defects to the Xiongnu and later advises a massive attack.

166 BC – The Xiongnu launch a major incursion into central China.

154 BC – The Han puts down the Rebellion of the Seven States.

141 BC – **Emperor Wu** of Han comes to power.

C. 139 BC – Explorer-diplomat **Zhang Qian** departs on a mission west seeking allies.

133 BC – Emperor Wu orders ambush of the Xiongnu at Mayi, effectively declaring war.

129 BC – Xiongnu launch an offensive.

129 BC – Led by **Li Guang** and **Wei Qing**, Han launches its first major campaign against the Xiongnu in more than seventy years.

127 BC – Wei Qing recaptures the Hexi Corridor.

126 BC – The *chanyu* **Yizhixie** comes to power.

125 BC – Yizhixie launches three-pronged assault into Chinese border provinces.

121 BC – Han general **Huo Qubing** inflicts devastating blows on the Xiongnu.

121 BC – A Xiongnu king surrenders to the Han, delivering lands and 40,000 men.

119 BC – Wei Qing leads the Han to victory in the Battle of Mobei ('Northern Desert').

108 BC – Han military actions claim Loulan and other key cities of the Western Territories.

110–105 BC – Peace bride Liu Xijun sent to the Wusun to secure alliance against Xiongnu.

C. 104 BC – **Princess Jieyou** replaces Liu Xijun after her death.

104 BC – **Li Guangli** marches west against the Dayuan kingdom in the War of the Heavenly Horses.

101 BC – **Li Guangli** defeats Dayuan.

87 BC – **Emperor Wu** dies.

71 BC – A combined Han-Wusun army defeats a Xiongnu force.

71 BC – Xiongnu attempt futile punitive campaign against Wusun.

60 BC – Outbreak of the Xiongnu Civil War.

59 BC – Office of Protector General of the Western Territories established.

56 BC – Xiongnu Civil War revolves around the factions of *chanyus* **Zhizhi** and **Huhanye**.

53 BC – Huhanye surrenders to the Han.

36 BC – A Han force supported by local allies defeats Zhizhi in the Western Territories.

AD 9 – Wang Mang becomes effective emperor, ending the Western Han dynasty. Chinese presence in the west fades and the Xiongnu factions reconstitute.

AD 23 – Wang Mang overthrown, ending the interregnum period.

AD 25 – Emperor Gengshi takes the throne, establishes the Eastern Han dynasty.

AD 33 – **King Xian of Yarkand** rebels against the Han, exerts power across the Western Territories.

AD 48 – Xiongnu partition into Northern and Southern factions.

AD 72 – After many years, the Han resumes expeditionary campaigns against the Xiongnu and prevails in the Battle of Yiwu.

AD 73 – Through the actions of the general **Ban Chao**, the Han starts to regain its foothold in the Western Territories.

AD 89 – Han general **Dou Xian** defeats the Northern Xiongnu, effectively ending the Han-Xiongnu War.

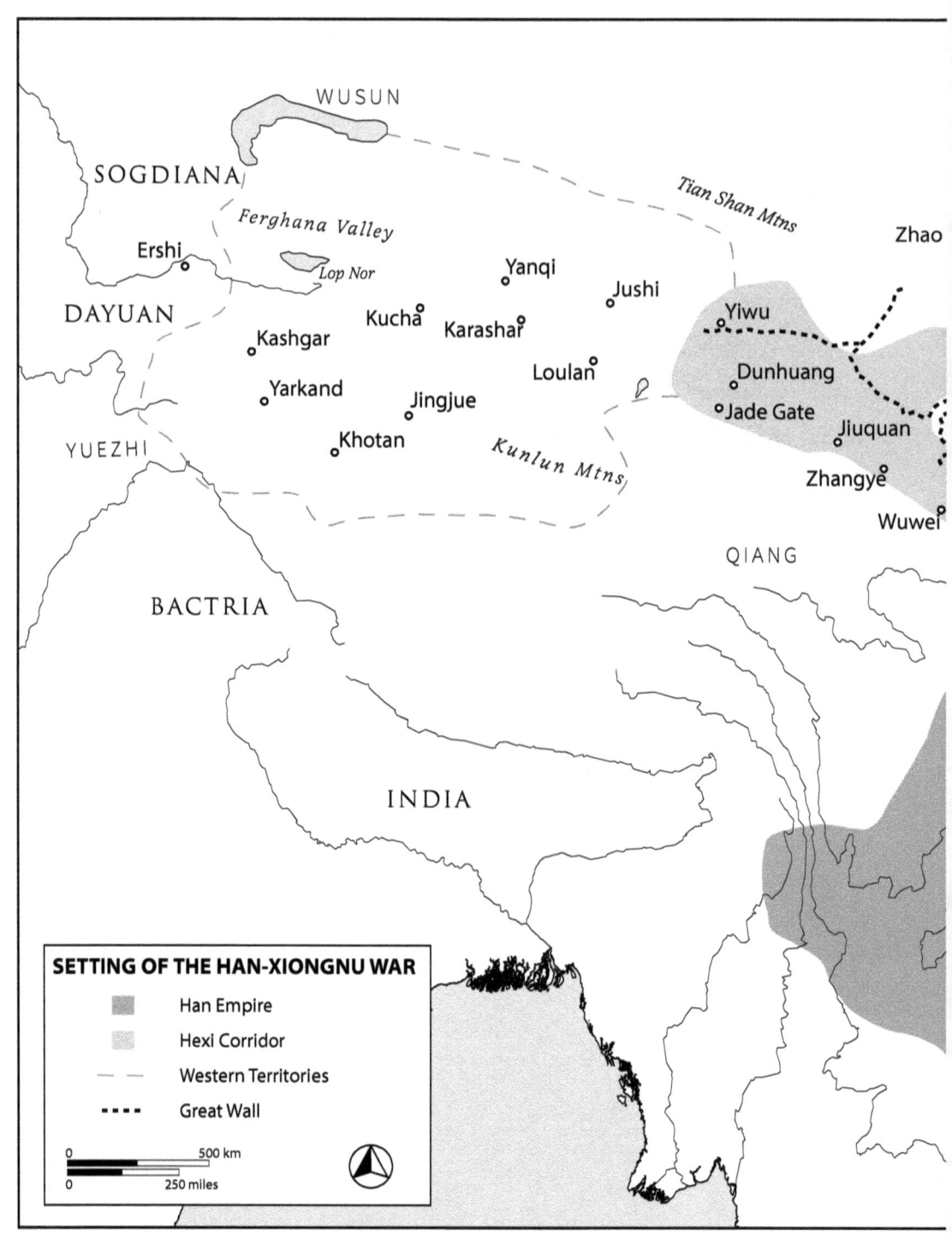

Map drawn by Tina Ross.

Prologue: A Misread Prophecy

While on an inspection tour of his realm in 215 BC, the thirty-second year of his reign, the first Emperor of China, Shi Huangdi, feared for his longevity. His project of uniting China under his boot heels as the Qin dynasty had barely reached its sixth year. So much remained to be done. In his travels he performed holy rites and offered sacrifices atop mountain peaks to ensure the health of his nascent empire and of his person, so that he may rule *tianxia*, 'all under Heaven'. The emperor also charged a scholar to venture out to sea in quest of the gods, that they might bestow upon him the secrets of immortality.

Over hundreds of years, the Qin dynasty had scrabbled its way from vassalage to ultimate power. Beginning in the ninth century BC the Qin people, considered semi-barbarian by other Chinese kingdoms, tended the horses of their stronger neighbouring states and protected their western marches, only to later emerge victorious in the bloody Warring States period (c. 475–221 BC). The Qin united the fractious kingdoms and established the first Chinese empire, concentrating its power in the person of Shi Huangdi. Guided by the pitiless philosophy of Legalism, which called for absolute rule as the only response in an immoral and venal world, he commanded a bureaucratic regime that verged on the totalitarian. Sima Qian (circa 145–circa 86 BC), a seminal chronicler of China's earliest history and a firsthand witness to some of the later Han dynasty's greatest events, remarked in his *Records of the Grand Historian* that the Qin emperor 'cracked his long whip and drove the universe before him'.[1] Through the emperor's unshaking resolve, he cobbled China together from an enormous landmass encompassing all manner of environments, from jungles and swamps to deserts and steppe, a vastness perhaps best summed up by the Chinese phrase 'in the south, by boat, and in the north, by horse'.

The ancient Chinese called the realm beyond their northern border 'Where the killing frosts come early', yet that would not dissuade them from yearning to seize it, particularly the Ordos Plateau. Roughly situated around the bend of the Yellow River, it was a fertile wellspring, capable of supporting agriculture and boasting handsome pasturage to raise the horses which were becoming so critical for the prosecution of warfare.

By the Chinese conception of the universe's organizing forces, this was also a region of *yin*, the female principle, with qualities associated with dampness, darkness, and obscurity, in contrast to the bright, clean and productive energy of *yang* male power, which naturally, by Chinese reckoning, rested in China. Thus these *yin* regions were ripe for invasion.

The trouble lay in the unfortunate fact that the Hu, a catch-all term for those considered barbarians by the Chinese, encompassing many tribes and civilizations, occupied the Ordos. In this case, the Hu were Xiongnu, a powerful confederacy of mounted nomadic pastoralists. That the Xiongnu homeland also exposed China's flank to attack just as the Qin was shoring up its territorial integrity, hastened the desire for subjugating it. The Qin capital of Xianyang stood in easy riding distance for the Xiongnu mounted warriors, unless the Qin seized the strategic territory out of their hands.

It would be a costly and dangerous campaign to mount – the lands inhospitable, especially to men not born to them, and the Xiongnu threat fearsome. The Qin emperor must have long considered the matter only to blanch in the face of the risk and expense. But then the divine seemed to chime in. The scholar he had dispatched to seek methods of immortality returned from his mission at sea and made his report: the gods had communicated with him, and they warned, 'Hu will destroy Qin'.[2]

Shi Huangdi interpreted this prophecy to mean he must eradicate the Xiongnu, or at least blunt the threat they posed by driving them far from striking range of Chinese lands. With the invasion sanctioned by the gods, the emperor turned to his trusted general Meng Tian, who assembled an army of 300,000. The Qin had revolutionized conscription and this capacity to mobilize gargantuan numbers of men would also serve China well in its expansionist campaigns – and rescue it time and again from shoddy decisions – in the coming decades and centuries.

Sima Qian's chronicle does not lavish detail about the 215 BC campaign against the Xiongnu, only recording that General Meng and his forces successfully drove the enemy far from the Ordos. For Meng to solidify his victory and establish lasting occupation of the region, he now turned his soldiers into engineers and builders, constructing the Great Wall. Composed primarily of rammed earth rather than stone, new sections of the Wall integrated natural features of the landscape to boost its effectiveness and reduce labour demands. Prior Chinese kingdoms had already raised walls in the region – their original purpose remains something of a mystery – and those still standing were repaired and joined up to the newly erected segments. In addition to establishing a contiguous defence and political border which stretched from the Tibetan Plateau to the coast of the Yellow Sea, this massive civil-military engineering project also planted an infrastructure which supported invasions for years to come. Paired with the massive roadbuilding projects into the region, the Great Wall offered reliable communication through the rugged, mountainous landscape. A lasting intellectual infrastructure also endured, which furnished a boundary marker for a slowly galvanizing collective identity for the Chinese – and suggested to them that they possessed both the right and the means to conquer and rule these lands.

Yet a common Chinese identity and the prospect of northern conquest faced a sudden danger of collapse. While touring his domains in 210 B.C., the emperor perished, most likely from ingesting alchemical potions brewed with mercury in his bid for immortality. His regime quickly teetered, with two sons competing for the throne, one of whom forged a letter which tricked the true heir to the throne into suicide and led to the death of General Meng. The usurping son's name? Prince Hu Hai.

The scholar who had voyaged across the sea for the secrets of eternal life relayed a prophecy, but its true meaning had eluded the emperor. The 'Hu' was not the Xiongnu, yet the prophecy of Hu destroying the Qin would be fulfilled, for Hu Hai would set in train the collapse of China's first empire. And those other Hu, the Xiongnu Empire, driven from their homeland, would one day return, to restore their territory and exact retribution on their southern neighbour.

Part One

Architects of War and Empire

Chapter I

Chanyu Modun (d. 174 BC): First Emperor of the Steppe

After their expulsion by the general Meng Tian from the Ordos, the *chanyu*, or ruler of the Xiongnu, Luanti Touman, led his people and their herds away in a hunt for new land. They were forced to trade the rich pasturage and cool streams of the Ordos – resources which made them pre-eminent across the region – for the hostile lands of bitter cold, wind, and enemies of northeast Asia. Yet out of these straits the Xiongnu would regain their strength, reclaim their former lands and seize new ones, and later cause the Chinese empire to tremble.

Xiongnu Origins and Identity

Xiongnu creation myth tells of a boy procreating with a she-wolf to birth their people. While this can clearly be dismissed, most details of their beginnings barely hover above the fog of time. Pursuing their period of origin will yield no clear answer, though it was likely in the third century BC (at least their first appearance in Chinese records suggests that). How much the Qin projection into Xiongnu lands precipitated their formation, or at least solidification, remains unclear, but at minimum it must have accelerated a process underway of discrete tribes setting aside grievances with one another in the name of collective survival, and to find wealth and glory together as a single power.

Even the name of these people defies easy investigation, as it is filtered and preserved through Chinese usage (with an ideographic writing system, foreign sounds were transliterated or ignored altogether in favour of assigning some other name more consistent with Chinese understanding or preference). The Chinese typically denigrated foreigners in their choice of characters, such as employing the semantic root for dog or animal in the names they selected. The Xiongnu name consists of two characters: *Xiong* meaning hidden, internal, and evil; and *nu*, meaning slave or child, and also bearing the feminine semantic root. (Incidentally, it is primarily by this similarity of name that a link between the Xiongnu and the later Huns is mooted, though scant evidence harmonizes with that passing phonological echo.)

Ethnic Composition and Languages

According to Sima Qian, the Xiongnu people could trace their origins to Chunwei, a ruler of the semi-legendary Xia dynasty (2700–1600 BC). By drawing a link between these barbarians and a Chinese ancestor, Sima Qian in effect made the Xiongnu distant cousins of the Chinese. Considering he did not follow strict genealogical evidence, why did he posit this? Possibly because it served Chinese imperial purposes at the time of his writing, through the suggestion Xiongnu could be absorbed and redeemed as a sort of wayward Chinese who simply required the right dose of civilization to tame, even if administered at the point of a sword.

Whether or not they carried the blood of distant Chinese monarchs, the overall ethnic composition of the Xiongnu clings to its lingering mystery. As a multi-ethnic, pluralistic confederacy of tribes, they did not conform to the identity of a distinct, monolithic group. Their features and appearances might have run the gamut, for over time they drew constituent peoples from a huge swathe of land stretching from the modern Mongolia and Manchuria to the east, Siberia to the north, and Tajikistan to the west, though most hailed from Mongolia. Given these sources, the Xiongnu must have blended Asian and Indo-European peoples into a wildly diverse polity.

Surely a variety of languages were spoken by its members. The common tongue of the Xiongnu court, governance, and intertribal communication is unknown, though possibly they turned to a Turkic or Iranian language for the purpose.

Religion

Just as their ethnic composition eludes easy definition, so too does their religion. As befits the multifarious origins of the Xiongnu people, no doubt several systems of faith guided its people. Yet one deity soared above all others: Tengri, the sky spirit. Trees and mountains held a sacred charge, for they stretched toward the heavens above. Nine levels of heavens were arrayed, each linked to a planet, and each of which housed a governing spirit; the one known was a war god, emblemized by a sword which possibly received sacrifices of human victims in its shrines. Sacrifices could be exchanged for the health of others – as we shall later see, a fugitive Chinese general even unwillingly gave his life that a *chanyu*'s mother might overcome her grave illness. Similarly, the shamanistic faith promoted militarism through the belief that slain foes became slaves upon the victorious warrior's eventual entry to the afterlife. To its warrior-adherents, Tengri could also bestow power and valour.

Unmoored to any particular place on Earth, it was a consummate nomadic religion – the sky, a functional infinity of space, was their spiritual landscape, encouraging broad roaming. This contrasted dramatically with the faith of many Chinese, among whose foundational gods was Shennong, the agricultural deity, and accordingly their conception of existence and their purpose in it was anchored to the earth.

Though Tengrism was light on dogma and free of an entrenched clergy, shamans played an instrumental role as intermediaries to Tengri and the pantheon of spirits. In Xiongnu myth, humans dramatically interacted with animals, even transformed into them – an apt theme, since animals stood at the heart of Xiongnu existence.

The 'Six Snouts'

The lives of the Xiongnu revolved around their animals, whose cycles set the rhythm of their keepers' days: shifting location as seasons changed to secure the finest pasturage for their livestock, tending to the foaling of their horses, and hunting game.

The primary animals were known as the 'six snouts': camels, goats, cows, and yaks, though especially horses and sheep. An immensely valuable resource, sheep provided meat, milk, fuel (from dung), wool, and skin. Reproducing quickly and, unlike other finicky herd animals, able to eat a wide array of plants, sheep made for ideal travelling partners to nomads on the move.

While sheep sustained the Xiongnu, the horse drove their daily, religious, and military lives. Probably first domesticated on the Russian steppe sometime between 4,000 and 3,000 BC, horses streamed outward, transforming the inhabitants of the steppe from people almost marooned by the vastness, condemned to eking out bare survival from near-desolate lands, to nomadic pastoralists who cultivated a specialized way of life based on raising herds that a sedentary existence could not support.

Critically for what would become a large-scale confederacy like the Xiongnu, the horse also shrank the immense steppe to a manageable size. Far-flung tribes and other groups, until this time all but divided by an impassable sea of grass, could readily interact. On horseback nomads could wander far, contacting distant people at a time when for all but the wealthiest and most courageous members of settled societies this was a great rarity. To the Xiongnu, a confederacy of people lacking the unifying factors of ethnicity and language, the horse allowed them to close the gaps which might otherwise have doomed unification as a futile enterprise.

When horses were first mounted for riding, or if they long simply pulled carts and chariots (in fact the chariot almost certainly was introduced to the Chinese by way of the steppe), remains under debate. That the Xiongnu were heirs to an equestrian tradition of more than a millennium and relied on these skills to forge an empire, is not in question. The horse filtered into all domains of life: the sheep herds they raised, the game animals they shot, and the raids they executed all depended on exquisite horsemanship.

This education began early. Young Xiongnu sat on the backs of sheep to learn the fundamentals of riding, and quickly progressed to ponies and smaller horses. And when paired with the composite bow that they virtually all mastered, the horse made the Xiongnu into formidable hunters – and warriors. Children took up the bow and learned the basics of shooting by killing small rodents and birds, and later larger animals. Shooting with discipline from the saddle, how to flush out quarry, communicating and working together to make their kills – all these lessons contributed to essential martial abilities which the Xiongnu called upon in the violent reconquest awaiting them.

Hardship – and Opportunity – in the Wasteland

When the Xiongnu leader Touman led his people into exile to the barren wastes at the foot of the Yin Mountains of Mongolia, they must have led a threadbare existence, their herds thinned by the poor pasturage, their security uncertain. This was a bleak time for the Xiongnu, and a dangerous time to be their leader.

Touman ruled as their *chanyu* (also written *shanyu*), perhaps meaning 'great' or 'son of the sky'. From this word derives the titles *khan* or *khagan* used by many other steppe peoples, including the Mongols. His clan was named the Luanti or Luandi. Touman's name is cognate with the Mongolian word *tumen*, a unit of 10,000 soldiers, a seminal number for the Xiongnu and many future tribal peoples (interestingly, in Chinese numerology it is also an important number which metaphorically represents a huge or even infinite number). As to Touman's pedigree, Sima Qian in his *Records of the Grand Historian* acknowledged the complexity of disentangling the Xiongnu lineage, as over many centuries and across a vast landscape the tribes divided and scattered, waxed and waned.

More than through an ideology or custom of rulership, a *chanyu* clung to his position based on his standing among the people. Suffering a loss of prestige and surely the power which accompanied it – for these were the attributes which rallied tribes to Touman's banner – could lead to crisis. Almost nothing is known of his life before he came into contact with Meng Tian and the

Qin, and thus entered the Chinese records. Yet whatever clout Touman achieved in earlier days, this undoubtedly suffered during the Xiongnu exile, when in addition to struggling to feed their herds and thus themselves, they were harried by longstanding tribal enemies. From the north threatened the Dingling people of Siberia, to their east massed the nomadic confederacy of the Donghu (a Chinese catch-all term for 'eastern barbarians') and in the west, the even more potent Yuezhi, whom the Xiongnu would clash with repeatedly in days to come. On the steppe it was common practice to make vassals of weaker rivals, and in this period the Donghu and Yuezhi both subjugated the once-mighty Xiongnu.

A key feature of vassalage, the holding of hostages to enforce good behaviour, played an important part in the transformation of the Xiongnu from a dejected rabble to an empire inspiring fear in its foes, on the steppe and in China. The Yuezhi compelled Touman to offer up a son as surety of compliance with their overlordship. While a humiliating token of Touman's fall from grace, this demand also presented the *chanyu* with a chance for an elegant solution to a problem which had gnawed at him. Here, through Sima Qian's narrative, Touman's son Modun enters the record. As the eldest son of the *chanyu*, Modun had been the crown prince, but among Touman's multiple wives and consorts he grew besotted with one in particular, and he began to favour a younger son he had with her as his successor. Possibly Modun had already cultivated a power base of his own and complying with the Yuezhi provided an expedient way for Touman to remove him without inflaming the young man's supporters. The *chanyu* sent him into his enemy's clutches – and based on what Touman was planning, he would have expected never to see his son again.

No record exists of the Xiongnu prince's experience in captivity. Whether on a day-to-day basis treated with civility or cruelty, his life hung in the balance should Touman ever attempt something as brazen as leading his soldiers against the Yuezhi. Though in a year unknown, Touman did just this, launching a sneak attack on them. At a stroke, Modun's life would have been forfeit.

Yet before the Yuezhi could execute the young man, he somehow stole a horse and made a daring escape. Heroically restored to his people, Modun's courage and skill won over his father, and in a display of Touman's new trust and affection, the prince was granted command of a cavalry force 10,000 strong.

Touman would come to regret that.

8   The Han-Xiongnu War, 133 BC–89 AD

The Rise of Modun

Quickly Modun took steps toward grasping a future outside his father's shadow and to buoy his standing among the Xiongnu. No doubt propelled by the tale of his derring-do, and able to tap the unit of men granted him by his father, Modun formed a corps of loyal followers and bodyguards. When his corps reached sufficient size, he began probing their dedication to his cause in a series of tests involving that quintessential activity of the Xiongnu: archery.

Modun took out his circle of supporters hunting, his quiver loaded with arrows which made a whistling noise in flight, designed to direct volleys. 'Send your arrows after mine,' he ordered, 'and if you do not, you will lose your head!'[1] First he shot at game, but then Modun targeted one of his own prized horses. Some in his retinue choked at taking such a shot; they had failed their leader's first test and Modun's punishment was harsh: summary execution.

Still it escalated, with Modun now choosing as his target one of his own beloved wives. Once more, some of his men could not go through with this; now knowing their loyalty was less than absolute, Modun put them to death. Then came the final test. In the previous hunting trips Modun had targeted his own horses and wives – those he by rights could destroy – but now, as he selected from his quiver another whistling arrow, he took aim at one of Touman's horses. Surely to harm any in the *chanyu*'s herd meant death, but not one of Modun's men failed to follow his lead. Now the prince could ready his next move.

Unlike many of the later cloistered monarchs of China, the *chanyu* put himself on display, leading in battle and delivering riches and glory. Touman's grip on his people depended on the stature he commanded among them. It is likely that dissension gathered against the man who presided over the Xiongnu exchange of life in the lands of sweet water and lush grasses of the Ordos to the parched plains of their exile. In such a setting Touman would struggle to project strength and reward his fighting men with a regular stream of rewards, the vital glue to cement his hold on the many tribes of his union. The expulsion from the Ordos presented Touman with a leadership quagmire but gifted an ambitious figure like his son Modun with opportunity. While reigning in the Ordos, perceived as the guarantor of comfort and glory, Touman was almost invulnerable. With the Xiongnu thrown to the winds and rocks of the northern wastes, and his own star ascendant, the moment had come for Modun to strike.

When he joined his father on a 209 BC hunting expedition, his loyalty-tested followers accompanied him. Amid the tracking of the game, Modun once again plucked a whistling arrow from his quiver, though this time he aimed at different prey. When he shot at his father, his men did not hesitate to also send their arrows.

At a stroke Modun decapitated the Xiongnu regime. Yet only speed and ruthlessness would enable him to shore up his position. He liquidated rival family members, such as his stepmother and the half-brother whose existence had been the cause of Modun's near-execution during his captivity with the Yuezhi, as well as other loyalists to Touman. No one remained to pose a credible challenge. Now Modun was *chanyu*, and his father's struggles to govern were his.

Leading a Fragmented Confederacy

The empire Modun now ruled was like a broken-down horse, sickly and ornery, the reins to guide it badly frayed. His people remained downtrodden and looked to him to lift their fortunes. Though positioned by birth for the throne, nonetheless he had to maintain his title through a mixture of charisma, intimidation and the ability to reward his followers with prestige and plunder. This emphasis on the individual rather than a dynasty eventually kneaded instability into the foundation of Xiongnu government, to the later despair of the Xiongnu and delight of the Chinese.

The Xiongnu did not organize in line with a clear ideology or a cult around a supreme leader, but rather as a sort of 'working group' fusing various factions, some of which surely nursed feuds among them. Yet Modun's boldness, in escaping the Yuezhi and in assassinating his father, likely both impressed and daunted his subjects. From his court at Long Cheng (a Chinese name meaning 'Dragon Fort'), located in central Mongolia, Modun engaged in all manner of negotiation and manoeuvre, toasting allies new and old with cups of horse blood to seal treaties, exchanging belts as devotions of loyalty, and sharing war spoils and other largesse. With allied kings, governors, and affiliated tribes to administer (and monitor), Modun had to find ways first to hold this complicated patchwork together and then to work toward shared survival and prosperity.

Xiongnu Political and Economic Structure

Scores of tribes had allied themselves under Touman. What caused these disparate groups to affiliate? While Qin unification had likely not been the impetus for the founding of the Xiongnu, perhaps after a century of fighting rivals and striving for power, the indisputable rise of an imperial Chinese power focused many nomads, ordinarily jealously guarding their independence, away from scattershot efforts and infighting, to confront the greater common enemy. Tribes effectively voted a *chanyu* in and so long as he brought advantage, they would swear continuing allegiance to their ruler.

At the head of the government stood the *chanyu*, whose succession to the throne followed a fraternal pattern: if the *chanyu* died and had a living brother, this man was the heir, not the *chanyu*'s son (challenges to this later spelled trouble for the empire). Modun turned to marquises of the Luanti royal family to run his imperial administration. Beneath him, two held highest rank: the Sage Kings of the Right (west) and Left (east), each governing roughly half the empire, with Right and Left subordinate kings further down the line; these individuals belonged to three aristocratic clans, the Xubu, Lan and Huyan. Prominent tribal leaders, numbering twenty-four, each commanded tumen units (each of 10,000 men, or at least a large number), and below that smaller units. Tribal chieftains, the lowest rung of power, received their lands from the *chanyu* and maintained close-to-autonomous rule over them.

All in all, it made for an unusual, and for the most part stable, structure of government, and a far cry from the tyrannical autocracy that characterized Qin dynasty rule in China. This flexible identity, as can be seen borne out over centuries, carried strengths and weaknesses, allowing former enemies to seamlessly merge with the Xiongnu but later, leading to the defection of key components of the empire.

A Xiongnu individual swore loyalty first to a tribal leader, that loyalty weakening as it extended up the hierarchy. This meant that aligning imperial and local priorities would be critical for Modun and all other *chanyus*. The Xiongnu thrived on motion, and keeping the people at rest might lead them to call the bonds linking a diverse polity into question, or even encourage criticism of the man who had placed himself above all others. One activity could perhaps transcend intertribal squabbles and tensions, reforging a sense of shared destiny and allowing Modun to solidify his rule: going on the warpath.

Taking the Fight to His Enemies

After consolidating his reign, Modun turned to neutralizing threats and settling scores. The newly reignited Xiongnu needed an enemy, and luckily or not, they were spoiled for choice. Just as the Qin had for his father, Modun could use other enemies, guilty of even fresher wrongs, to reap political hay. Those nearest to them would serve to ginger up his people and put his army through its paces before seeking mightier prey.

Crushing the Donghu

Modun targeted his most immediate threat first: the Donghu, or Eastern Barbarians. Most likely a confederation whose principal members were the nomadic Wuhuan and Xianbei peoples, they controlled territory east of the Xiongnu and likely had effectively made vassals of them after the expulsion from the Ordos. Already Modun had dealings with them. After he became *chanyu*, the Donghu sent envoys, not to congratulate him on his new position but to reinforce their overlordship by demanding he gift to them a famously magnificent horse which had belonged to his father.

Here came an early test of Modun's resolve. His advisors pleaded with him to make a stand and refuse. But Modun was playing a long game, taking the measure of the Donghu and preparing the ground for a strike against them. He responded that the Donghu 'are our neighbours, why bother to lose harmony with them over a single horse'.[2] The Donghu envoys rode home with the animal, nettling Modun's advisors at such a display of subservience. Were they wrong to have supported this weakling?

Believing the *chanyu* cowed, the next Donghu envoy requested he take away one of his consorts. 'They are our neighbours, why bother losing our accord over a woman,' he responded to his advisors' qualms.[3] Then came the greatest test yet of his leadership, and of Modun's tolerance. Emboldened by the *chanyu*'s previous submissions, the Donghu now staked a claim to a parcel of uninhabitable land in the Gobi Desert which belonged to the Xiongnu.

Uninterested in that barren waste, the *chanyu*'s advisors suggested he not bother contesting this violation. 'Those lands are the foundation of our nation,' he angrily replied, promptly executing those in his circle willing to surrender territory without a fight.[4] And now Modun's masterful subterfuge would come to full flower.

Rallying his warriors – and threatening execution of those who tarried in joining him – he launched an attack on the unsuspecting Donghu. Lulled into dropping their guard after his previous accommodation of their outrageous demands, the enemy had not been on a standing for war. Modun and his forces landed a devastating blow against them, killing and enslaving many. For their leader, Modun reserved a special treatment: his skull was repurposed as the *chanyu*'s drinking vessel – a common practice among steppe peoples, these cups were used as politically charged symbols when sealing alliances.

Modun shattered the Donghu confederation, its component tribes strewn across the region like a panicked herd. One day they would bring great suffering upon the Xiongnu, but for now he defanged this enemy who had once humiliated his people. Now, to an even mightier foe and greater rewards.

Campaigning Against the Yuezhi

With their flank no longer vulnerable to the Donghu, Modun pushed his people to the west in a bid to reclaim the Ordos. Curiously, he did not find Chinese military or settlers there, but rather his old captors he had once escaped, the Yuezhi. The Qin's occupation of the Ordos in 215 BC had shrivelled away with the collapse of the dynasty and in the absence of the Xiongnu, the Yuezhi had seized it.

Most likely an Indo-European people, Chinese chroniclers recorded that the Yuezhi bore many similar characteristics to the Xiongnu, which might suggest that they too practised nomadic pastoralism and fought primarily as mounted archers. With soldiers numbering 100,000 or more, the Yuezhi posed even more of a danger than the Donghu. Already they had withstood Touman's earlier sneak attack upon them.

Though they must have fought ferociously to keep their fertile lands with abundant pasturage and water, circa 203 BC Modun attacked and drove the Yuezhi out of the Ordos. Through his vision and skill at war, Modun led his people to reoccupy the lands that the Chinese had banished them from.

Bracing Against China

In a few short years of his rule, Modun had gloriously lifted the fortunes of his people. His standing could hardly seem to rise higher after the reconquest of the Ordos. Yet now he accepted the duty of protecting a region lusted for by both nomadic and settled peoples. The Yuezhi had not been destroyed, though Modun had likely damaged them enough that they could not send their riders at the Xiongnu again for some time. It was China, who had driven off the Xiongnu in 215 BC, which had proved they could mobilize the strength to challenge Modun.

Though the Qin had fallen, Modun likely saw the threat from the south, after a new regime came to power, as all but inevitable. The Ordos simply proved too attractive a target. Thus, purely for reasons of defence, Modun would have been wise to gird for war. Internal politics factored in as well. He was riding high, yet the nature of Xiongnu society was such that an external threat kept them focused and united. The Chinese could give new lifeblood to his fledgling empire; the threat they offered in turn strengthened the sinews of the confederacy. A world without the Qin actually meant danger for the Xiongnu, whereas the rise of a new Chinese dynasty striving for unity instead held great promise.

Soon Modun and his growing empire would face an opponent with the face of a dragon.

Chapter II

Liu Bang (256–195 BC): From Rebel to Emperor

It all began with a rainstorm.

In 208 BC, Liu Bang, a petty law enforcement official of the Qin dynasty, who 'had a prominent nose and a dragon-like face, with beautiful whiskers on his chin and cheeks', had been tasked with delivering a gang of convicts to a government site.[1] They were sentenced to perform hard labour in the construction of the mausoleum of Shi Huangdi, the emperor who had died two years earlier from probable mercury poisoning. During the transit, some of the prisoners escaped, and when heavy rain slowed his progress, Liu faced a choice: carry on, to deliver the remaining prisoners late and then risk the severe and perhaps lethal recriminations of his superiors – or rebel against the Qin.

China paid grave costs in order to unite her long-warring kingdoms. Shi Huangdi had embarked on a draconian spree of standardization, making the language, weights and measures, road widths and more conform to common rules. This stoked tension and the embers of resistance were poised to flare. The governing philosophy of the Qin, known as Legalism, which began to be practised in the fourth century BC, stressed that a sovereign's subjects, who are by nature selfish and petty, must be coerced into serving their state and ruler. Proponents of Legalism rejected the Confucians, who advocated the moral cultivation of individuals that they may better yield to the natural hierarchy of society; a major Legalist thinker stated that farming and war make a nation powerful, and indeed, for Qin China these domains went hand in hand, the common people were cogs in a massive machine, their labour to be exploited, their sentiments closely monitored.

Such hardnosed policy had made the Qin briefly formidable, but at root frail. At this stage, the Chinese empire reeled at the brink of collapse. Qin authority had been so embedded in Shi Huangdi's personal rule that on his death in 210 BC his retainers feared for the dynasty's prospects enough to conceal this dangerous tiding. They transported his body back to the capital in a coffin filled with aromatic herbs and dried fish to disguise the rotting stench, lest some onlookers understand their way of life now hung in the balance.

The fissures in the regime quickly widened, the people fed up with corvée labour and unfeeling policies, so that when a mutiny broke out, the 'whole world gathered like a cloud, answered like an echo to a sound … and followed after them as shadows follow a form', and the people 'rose up together and destroyed the house of Qin'.² Against this backdrop of rebellion, Liu Bang made his choice about whether to remain a dutiful officer of the empire.

'Gentlemen, all go away,' he told the convicts as he removed their fetters. 'From this time on I too will abscond.'³ Some of them, seeing better prospects of survival, or perhaps a chance at something far greater, rewarded his gesture by becoming his followers (a humble start which in some ways parallels Modun's early gestures towards power after escaping captivity with the Yuezhi). With these followers Liu went on to build a coalition, expanding his power base along the Han River.

An earthy, unrefined man, likely of peasant origin, in his early life Liu showed more interest in hard drinking than hard work. He loved banquets, playing the zither, singing, and the company of women. Yet as a Qin official, despite his likely illiteracy, he would have been schooled in the practices of bureaucracy and organization. He also boasted the common touch and a willingness to draw from a wide pool of talent – later, one of his chief generals was a former dog butcher. Liu recognized his limitations and found the right people to compensate for them, a quality which served him well in his coming clashes.

Battling His Way to the Dragon Throne

An effective battlefield commander, Liu led his fledgling army against the vestiges of the Qin military, though the empire's fate was written. In 206 BC at Xianyang, the Qin capital, Liu accepted the surrender of its monarch and spared his life. But the rebellion against the Qin had prompted states which had been united to splinter; now eighteen kingdoms jockeyed for position in the aftermath of the imminent victory. The struggle settled into two states vying for ultimate rule, in what is known as the Chu-Han Contention: Liu Bang's domain situated around the Han River, and the far larger state of Chu, led by a duke, and later king, Xiang Yu.

In their struggle against the Qin the two men began as nominal allies. Before a state of war existed between them, they met for a banquet at Hongmen ('Swan Goose Gate'), near Xiangyang. Xiang Yu recognized in Liu a dangerous enemy and thought to assassinate him at the soonest opportunity. To accompany the lavish dishes and free-flowing liquor, Xiang Yu charged his cousin to entertain the guests with a sword dance – a cunning pretext to allow an armed man to approach Liu and land a killing thrust.

But whenever the would-be assassin closed on his target, Xiang Yu's uncle, with whom Liu had cultivated a personal relationship, would step in and block the attack. The banquet ended without bloodshed, but the battlelines were indelibly drawn and later that year war broke out. Liu often found himself on the back foot, his army typically outnumbered by Xiang Yu's forces by four to one. Yet Liu, flexible and cunning, made great use of circumstances and most of all, the people whom he encountered. He formed alliances and rallied nobles and others to his banner by promising enfeoffments (grants of land in return for service) – even, when caught between two armies, using this scheme to flip one of their generals to his own banner. And unlike the arrogant, punctilious Xiang Yu, Liu recognized his shortcomings and willingly delegated tasks to those superior.

Throughout the Chu-Han Contention Liu made a series of narrow escapes. At one point nearly captured by Xiang Yu forces, he raced away in a cart, prepared to abandon his children to improve his chances, until a subordinate prevailed upon him not to make such a disgraceful sacrifice. In another incident, Liu and Xiang stood facing each other, a gorge yawning between them. The latter challenged him to single combat, but Liu – perhaps recognizing Xiang Yu as the stronger fighter in single combat – instead shouted an exhaustive list of the other's crimes. To this Xiang made blunt reply, sending a crossbow bolt winging into Liu's chest.

Here Liu demonstrated his keen political instincts and the recognition that an effective leader must also be a performer. Biting back the pain, he feigned that it was nothing but a trifling wound, crying out, 'The bastard hit me in the finger!'[4] In this we see his canny wiles as a commander, not wanting either the enemy or his own men to learn the gravity of his injury. He then made a show of walking around his camp to further convince his men, until the pain grew too great and he hid himself away to recover.

Though Liu's armies achieved victories, the war came to an apparent stalemate; Liu and Xiang agreed to an armistice. Yet Liu smelled blood. He wooed a key ally, the general Han Xin who in 202 BC attacked an unsuspecting Xiang at the Battle of Gaixia, fully encircling him. Rather than fall into enemy hands, Xiang Yu took his own life.

Liu had drawn on his cunning and, vitally, his men to triumph in the Chu-Han Contention. At a victory banquet, he posed a question to his followers: 'Why is it that I won possession of the world and Xiang Yu lost?' They replied because unlike the stingy Xiang Yu, he rewarded his followers generously, doling out enfeoffments and plunder. Agreeing with this, Liu also added:

When it comes to sitting within the tents of command and devising strategies that will assure us victory a thousand miles away, I am no match for Zhang Liang. In ordering the state and caring for the people, in providing rations for the troops and seeing to it that lines of supply are not cut off, I cannot compare to Xiao He. In leading an army of a million men, achieving success with every battle and victory with every attack, I cannot come up to Han Xin. These three are all men of extraordinary ability, and it is because I was able to make use of them that I gained possession of the world. Xiang Yu had his one Fan Zeng, but he did not know how to use him and thus he ended as my prisoner.[5]

Liu turned to others to compensate for his shortcomings, something Xiang Yu could not find it in himself to do. While able to lead on the battlefield, his talents truly shone as a manager, testament, perhaps, to his upbringing in the Qin government structure. Corralling the right talent, he laid the groundwork for a bureaucratic, militarized empire patterned on the previous regime.

China would need such instruments to tap all available resources, for while Chu and Han spent years in civil war, the Xiongnu had not been sitting idle. With a vacuum in the north, they recaptured much of the territory they had lost to the Qin, and in so doing reclaimed their earlier fighting spirit as well.

Uniting Former Enemies, Confronting a New One

On 28 February 202 BC Liu Bang became emperor, sitting on the Dragon Throne and adopting the ruling name Gaozu ('Great Founder'). The minor bureaucrat had transformed to the 'Son of Heaven' – a title stemming from the Zhou dynasty (c. 1046–256 BC) concept of the 'Mandate of Heaven' which ordained the sovereign's divine right to rule. Yet the immediate fragmentation after the Qin collapse, with states resisting imperial unification in favour of independence, showed the scale of challenge Liu faced.

His dynasty would be named the Han, after the Han River in central China. Liu opted to build his capital in the heart of the old empire, across a river from the Qin capital of Xianyang. His city was Chang'an ('Eternal Peace'), located near the modern city of Xi'an. Perhaps, with the memory of the Qin driving the Xiongnu from the Ordos region still relatively fresh, he underestimated the severity of the Xiongnu threat. Or, rather, it was quite the opposite, and he wished to be situated for mounting an attack on the north should it become necessary or appealing.

Further, by seating the capital in its strategic location, the emperor could keep an eye on the relations between the Xiongnu and his own subjects, some of whom hoped to rebel and sought allies in the nomadic empire.

The Xiongnu Move In

Forged in the ashes of the Qin and the war with Chu, in some ways the incipient Han dynasty resembled the Xiongnu empire, a web of complex vassalages, appanages, far-flung subjects and allies of brittle allegiance. The Chinese states had chafed under Qin rule and did not clamour for a return to centralized control, preferring a reversion to feudalism. Thus soon after taking the throne, Liu Bang faced revolts from his kings and fief lords. The Xiongnu, newly strengthened by claiming the Ordos and the prestige and power that brought, waded into this domestic political landscape. Vassal states now under Han rule seeking to align with the burgeoning Xiongnu presented a keen danger to the imperium, especially as the terms of alignment would surely be less onerous than absolute fealty to the newly seated emperor. Already in 197 BC the Han had thwarted an attempted rebellion in which the marquis Chen Xi attempted to league with the nomads.

Kingdoms and appanages at China's borders, in easy communication with the Xiongnu, and with whom they historically had trade and other contact, posed a particular danger. With Xiongnu backing, these polities might strengthen enough to pose a challenge to the unstable Dragon Throne. And indeed, fief lords and Han-affiliated kings faced a dilemma, unable to predict whether the Xiongnu might outlast the Han, still in its infancy and highly vulnerable to risks, from without and within.

To the weak, newly formed Han regime, the Xiongnu represented both a grave military threat unto themselves, and a potential ally to rebels. In fact, in an early encounter, a Chinese general lost territory to the Xiongnu but then fled to the emperor, for which the failed general earned a promotion, as he demonstrated loyalty to Liu Bang rather than going over to the enemy. So, at all costs, Liu sought to avoid a clash with the Xiongnu, striving instead to consolidate his rule. Already they had participated in Chinese political life, perhaps for decades, with Xiongnu potentially having served as allies or mercenaries during the Warring States period.

One early stirring of trouble came from the state of Han (a distinct polity not to be confused with the Han dynasty) and its king, Han Xin (somewhat confusingly, not the same Han Xin who defeated Xiang Yu at the Battle of Gaixia). Han Xin's lands in the northwest abutted Xiongnu territory and from Mayi ('the City of Horses'), he could easily communicate with the nomads.

18   The Han-Xiongnu War, 133 BC–89 AD

Trouble came in 200 BC when the Xiongnu appeared to mount an attack upon King Xin of Han's land. Yet the emperor suspected this was only a ploy for the king and the Xiongnu to link up. Whether this had indeed been a subterfuge all along which the emperor shrewdly detected, or because his suspicions brought this about, Han Xin could not risk remaining in China and he defected to the nomads. Despite the emperor's reluctance, the defection forced his hand against the Xiongnu. Liu Bang called up his army.

The Battle of Baideng (White Peak)

The early Han army adopted the doctrines and practices of its Qin predecessor, including massive mobilization through conscription. The Qin had accomplished this through a combination of a vast bureaucratic machine running censuses and maintaining scrupulous records, and the termination of the feudal system. Peasants gained their own land, which made them owe taxes and service to the state rather than to their local lords. This inherited capacity meant Liu could assemble a force of 320,000 men in his campaign to punish the Xiongnu for meddling in Chinese affairs. And although he now wore an emperor's raiment, he did not shrink from dirtying his hands, for Liu had earned his stripes in battle and now took personal command of his army as they marched toward Mayi.

The Han lacked substantial numbers of horses (historically, China was bedevilled by a lack of the animals, which would drain their fighting capacity for decades, and later the Han launched campaigns to address that very problem). Because of this, their cavalry would be a pittance compared to the effectively all-mounted force of the Xiongnu – a massive handicap. Chariots provided command-and-control functions and likely operated as mobile platforms for archers. But the army's core strength lay in infantrymen equipped with swords and spears forged from durable, high-quality iron, and ranks of crossbowmen operating state-of-the-art machines. Especially in these early days of Han rule, the majority of these soldiers probably lacked intensive training, though a certain number of veterans from Liu Bang's campaigns would surely have been fielded, at the very least to reinforce green troops. Yet all of his soldiers and officers could be considered green when it came to fighting a mounted nomadic army, as they soon discovered.

The army progressed towards Mayi in what is now China's Shanxi Province. Liu rode in the lead, his gargantuan infantry force trailing. Having raised such a huge army, Liu Bang must have been confident he could smash the elusive enemy, no matter how devious their tactics. Nevertheless, he dispatched reconnaissance teams to assess Xiongnu strength. They reported finding only weak enemy soldiers in the field. Heartened, the emperor charged on with his army. He came into contact with Xiongnu elements and the successful engagements confirmed the earlier intelligence delivered by his scouts – in a few skirmishes he prevailed and put the enemy to flight. On horses and in chariots, Liu and some of his men sped after them. His haste meant the main body of his lumbering, foot-soldier army trailed well behind him. But the emperor, an inveterate gambler, knew when to seize a chance that might well escape him, so he chased Modun's army through the mountains. Drawn ever deeper into the freezing heights, frostbite ate at Liu's soldiers, twenty to thirty per cent of them losing their fingers. Yet the fighting emperor went on with his advance units, his main infantry corps still far behind.

Then the Xiongnu materialized, in their hundreds of thousands. Perhaps only then did Liu Bang understand the finely crafted trap he had rushed into – which had been the *chanyu* Modun's plan all along. The pitiful soldiers Liu Bang's scouts discovered and dismissed? These Modun had deliberately displayed as decoys to bait the Chinese pursuit. The Xiongnu had masterfully denied battle, stringing the Han forces out, far from their base of support with supply lines thin – and then had raced in and encircled Liu. Now the emperor of China was all but held hostage.

Cut off from reinforcements and provisions, the situation was bleak. Some of Liu's generals began straying to the Xiongnu. How the emperor freed himself from this siege remains a mystery, with one later source, *The Book of Han*, claiming Liu Bang followed a 'secret plan' which could not be revealed. Sima Qian records the emperor dispatched an envoy bearing gifts for Modun's consort, who then went to the *chanyu* and asked:

> Why should the rulers of these two nations make such trouble for each other? Even if you gained possession of the Han lands, you could never occupy them, and the ruler of the Han may have his guardian deities as well as you. I beg you to consider the matter well![6]

Her counsel perhaps struck a chord, for it spoke to an underlying weakness of Xiongnu military power: while it might prevail in the field, it lacked the numbers and capacity to hold conquered lands. And further, it framed an overriding dilemma for Modun: what was the value of crushing the enemy wholesale? At this stage, the Han offered no existential threat to the Xiongnu and, indeed, perhaps a fallen China might also mean tribal enemies of the Xiongnu could come to the fore, for China offered a buffer against them. More fundamentally, if the Han were now brought to their knees, inevitably the Chinese states would erupt into civil war. And that would make them an unreliable payer.

For Modun devised another way to claim victory from the Han without destroying them. The Chinese had wealth, and this could be exploited. These conditions led to Liu's escape from encirclement and the birth of a policy which for the next seven decades kept the two empires from all-out war.

Buying His Freedom, Saddling the Han's Future

Liu Bang rode away from Baideng and returned to an empire poised for a sea change. He had bought his freedom at Baideng, and in the aftermath as Xiongnu attacks continued nipping at Chinese lands, the emperor sought to find a way to buy continuing peace. *Heqin*, or the marriage alliance, would now govern relations between the two lands, underlaying a fragile peace. Simply, the Han provided goods, luxuries, and princesses or royal concubines to the *chanyu* and his court, in return for the *chanyu* acknowledging the Great Wall as the border between their empires and ordering no further attacks on China.

With the marriage alliance in effect, China, for the first time, recognized a foreign power as its equal – and the emperor, at least diplomatically, joined the *chanyu* to his imperial family. Their relations would have been even more direct, with Liu Bang first considering sending his own daughter, until Liu's wife's pleas won him over and a royal woman of lesser rank filled the role instead. All this was a bitter pill for the emperor to swallow, yet he had enemies closer to home demanding attention. Revolts continued to frustrate the Han, and the emperor, no longer a young man, still rode into the field to meet his challengers.

In a battle against a rebelling vassal king in 195 BC, Liu Bang took an arrow wound. This time, he could not feign indifference to it as he had after being shot by Xiang Yu, for it grew infected. After examining him a doctor explained he had escaped a mortal wounding. Liu replied, 'Wearing the clothes of a commoner, I took on the world with my three-foot sword. Was this not my destiny? Heaven shall decide my fate.'[7] On the first of June Heaven spoke, and the first emperor of the Han was no more.

To his wife and young son, he bequeathed his rickety empire. To future generations, he passed forward the debt of payments to the Xiongnu and the continued smearing of imperial prestige. Yet the marriage alliance allowed the regime to right itself and husband its strength for the day when the Han could take to the field and meet their foe again.

Chapter III

Emperor Wu of Han (156–87 BC): The 'Martial Emperor'

I am a forlorn king living in the damp and marshy swamps in the north. I grew up among my herd and cattle. Every time I rode to the border of Han, I wished to visit the heartland of the Middle Kingdom [China]. Now, Your Majesty, you are all alone without a spouse. Since the two of us are both unhappy ... why don't we get together to share what we both miss?[1]

In 192 BC Chanyu of the Xiongnu Modun scandalized the Han court by sending that prurient letter to the empress dowager, a widow of Liu Bang. To make a sexual jest with a member of the Han royal family put in stark relief what a new reality existed between the empires of the Xiongnu and the Chinese. After Liu and his army retreated from the Battle of Baideng and licked their wounds, his dynasty just managed to survive intact, but now surely smarted at the barbs to their dignity. And for a regime still squelching dissent, dignity was vital to their imperial authority and thus the continued survival of the realm.

The Marriage Alliance and its Discontents

The marriage alliance policy went into effect in 198 BC. All manner of goods but mostly luxuries, such as silk and liquor, crammed into trains of carts trundling north. While these gifts could be delivered without direct imperial involvement, sometimes the emperor honoured the recipients by inviting them to grand receptions, and personally serving extravagant meals and bestowing wondrous gifts – something the Son of Heaven would consider unthinkable with virtually any Chinese subject.

Why did the Han endure such tarnishing of their prestige and standing among their own people? For one, it neatly divided the imperial domains, as Emperor Wen of Han, the son of Liu Bang, who lived 203–157 BC and ruled from 180 BC until his death, wrote to the *chanyu* in a letter of 162 BC:

the land north of the Great Wall, where men wield the bow and arrow, was to receive its commands from the *Shanyu*, while that within the wall, whose inhabitants dwell in houses and wear hats and girdles, was to be ruled by us.²

Ostensibly, a clear border existed between the empires, though that line was firmer in the Chinese imagination than in reality.

The marriage alliance intended to forbid attacks by the Xiongnu and, quite simply, the Han were not yet in a position to answer militarily to incursions. Yet by Chinese reckoning, the alliance could be used as a weapon against its supposed beneficiaries.

False Faith in the Alliance's Offensive Capacity

T'ai Kung's Six Secret Teachings, a Chinese strategic manual from the Warring States period, suggested that toward an enemy, one should 'support his dissolute officials in order to confuse him. Introduce beautiful women and licentious sounds in order to befuddle him. Send him outstanding dogs and horses in order to tire him.'³ While the marriage alliance with the Xiongnu occurred in a later era, some Han officials thought along the same lines, believing that the grant of high-status Chinese women, luxury goods, and more could be considered strategic gifts to weaken and steer an enemy perceived as driven solely by bestial appetites. These came to be known as the 'Five Baits', in which the Han should offer

> elaborate clothes and carriages in order to corrupt their eyes; to give them fine food in order to corrupt their mouth; to give them music and women in order to corrupt their ears; to provide them with lofty buildings, granaries and slaves in order to corrupt their stomach.⁴

Not only would these luxuries distract and corrupt the Xiongnu recipients, but perhaps, in the Chinese view, it might enlighten the barbarians on the splendours of higher culture. The Xiongnu were a 'raw' people, lacking the proper 'cooking' which only civilization – of which none was more refined than China – could provide. Just as Sima Qian drew a link between the Xiongnu and a distant Chinese ancestor, many believed the Xiongnu could be brought around with shrewd enticements.

Another alleged Chinese weapon concealed within the exchange, and guided by similar logic, was the perceived promise that half-Chinese children – the offspring of the married-off Chinese princesses and consorts and their *chanyu* husbands – would mature and become Xiongnu rulers, then show their filial loyalty to their motherland, compelling a sort of biological loyalty to the Han. This allegiance of bloodline, however, failed to overcome the experience of spending their entire lives as Xiongnu.

These were the theories behind the marriage alliance, anyhow, or at least the rationalizations by which the Han could tolerate its continuation. While attempts to spin Han advantage mostly failed, the arrangement did bring the two empires into contact, allowing the Chinese to gather intelligence about their enemy and, later, exploit fissures within Xiongnu society. The alliance also provided a foundation for Xiongnu subordinates, inspired by greed or because they had run afoul of their *chanyu*, to find a lifeline in the Han by defecting to them.

The diplomatic treaty stressed the Han treasury and its status with its people, though so long as this kept Chinese borders secure they could accept this. There was one problem, however – it did not work.

Misconstruing the Xiongnu

For the *chanyu*, the marriage alliance granted incredible prestige. With the inflow of treasure he could reward his political allies and rise in stature. This wealth of course boosted the *chanyu*'s eminence among his people, for he could dole it out to reward allies in the confederacy and motivate those less committed. Yet another source of imperial prestige for him came in the form of Chinese princesses to marry ('princess' was a flexible term, as sometimes the women were imperial concubines or, as we shall see in Chapter IX, disgraced lesser aristocrats).

Yet Modun's loose hold on his people also made the alliance fundamentally unstable, degrading the value of the arrangement to the Han. Treaty violations in the form of significant raids occurred with alarming regularity. These actions could prompt a revisiting of the marriage alliance terms, essentially a negotiation technique, although in some cases these raids might have been defensive in nature, checking the expansion of Chinese influence and occupation into the north. Chinese settlements along the border meant locals did not scrupulously respect imperial policy delineating the Great Wall as the boundary between Xiongnu and Han, especially if trade with the Xiongnu offered handsome profit. A Chinese saying, 'Heaven is high and the emperor far away', captures the probable mentality.

The realities of Xiongnu governance and a failure of Chinese understanding of what bound and drove a people so geographically close but culturally distant hobbled the marriage alliance's efficacy from the start. Just as the *chanyu* required raids and warfare to reward his followers, so did tribal chieftains who, while affiliated with the empire, might not receive the *chanyu*'s largesse which they could then in turn trickle down to their men. And thus these tribes launched their own raids, with no coordination with the *chanyu* or other imperial authority, and therefore not a 'state-level' military action.

Perhaps the Han should have shown more perspective, as their own troubles stemmed largely from restive vassals. In any event, these violations promoted clamour for war among some Han officials, yet still the empire stood ill-prepared for a large-scale clash. For now, China had no choice but to absorb these raids.

A Risk to Imperial Unity

Xiongnu incursions not only demoralized and bled assets from China, but with the imperial state still shaky, presented potential opportunities for border governors to ally with the raiders. States under the Han had to be closely watched when attacks occurred lest they link with the Xiongnu and rebel, as had happened with King Han Xin, leading to the Battle of Baideng. Even after the raiders galloped away through the smoke of sacked towns, satiated from their raids or driven off by a Han reaction force, the danger was not past – for states only nominally sworn to the Han emperor might exploit the turmoil and challenge imperial authority.

Han society, essentially totalitarian, supplied compelling reasons for some to defect. Those who faced potential sanction by the government might have found themselves at a fork much like Liu Bang did, when he opted to rebel rather than suffer the judgement of his Qin superiors. Xiongnu society, on the other hand, with an identity which was effectively built around the task of common survival, rather than upholding a particular ideology or dogma, was dangerously permeable and even welcoming of outsiders. Thus the Han sought to ensure its subjects were deafened to the call, and if some Chinese did hear it, they must be stopped from acting on it.

Buying Time – and Weapons

Treaty violations notwithstanding, the alliance did enable the still-developing Han dynasty to put its house in order and address internal imperial challenges, such as an attempted coup in 180 BC. And by avoiding war with the Xiongnu, the empire could focus on building national strength, principally through farming. 'Agriculture is the basis of the empire,' decreed Emperor Wen. 'Among the endeavours of man, none is more important.'[5] This in turn swelled imperial treasuries, allowed for the Han to stockpile weaponry, obtain horses, and otherwise expand military capacity toward the day they repaid the Xiongnu for the humiliations of Baideng, and the shame which accompanied each transfer of Chinese wealth to the barbarians.

The marriage alliance also restrained the Han from leaping into a war they were not yet ready to fight. Some imperial advisors noted that, while the annual payments cost them dearly, still they paled in comparison to the costs of fielding armies, especially if they were lost through combat, starvation, exposure, or defections. And what of the costs if the Han went to war and lost?

Over the years Han society steadied itself. The reigns of Emperor Wen and his son Jing (188–141 BC, ruled 157 BC until his death) gained renown for their frugality and temperance, and avoiding war surely played a great part in that. The philosophy of Confucius, a sage of the fifth century BC, penetrated more deeply into the culture, its stressing of obedience to authority and carefully delineated social relationships moulded by hierarchy useful to dynastic rulers. Confucianism would also play an increasing part in China's military culture. This philosophy and other Chinese traditions highlighted a dichotomy in Chinese thought of *wen* and *wu*. *Wen*, a word with broad meanings, encompassing civics, culture, literature, and language, dealt with aspects of government and regulation guided by social virtues and self-cultivation. *Wu* corresponded to militarism and the application of force; Legalism, the governing philosophy of the Qin, with a strong residue still present in Han society, more naturally aligned with *wu*. While Confucianism did not advocate pacificism, it looked askance at military action, and anti-war forces within the Han imperial administration invoked this in their arguments favouring the continuation of a status quo with the Xiongnu.

Growing Threats

Circa 174 BC another letter arrived at the Chinese court from the puckish Chanyu Modun: 'Praise to the benevolence of Heaven, having endowed our warriors with great spirits and making our warhorses robust we have completely vanquished the Kingdom of Yuezhi.'[6] Gloatingly he went on, listing other kingdoms to the west which had been defeated or surrendered to the Xiongnu and fallen under the steppe empire's suzerainty.

This victory came on the heels of the Xiongnu, circa 180 BC, besting another steppe people, the Wusun who occupied lands neighbouring Yuezhi territory around the Qilian Mountains (later in the war, the Wusun loomed large). The marriage alliance with China obviously heaped benefits on the Xiongnu, which then compounded the wealth and status enough to attract strong tribes, buy arms, and distribute rewards which forged the confederacy into the predominant power on the steppe.

With Xiongnu possession of the Ordos, they now also controlled the Hexi ('West of the Yellow River') Corridor. This strip of semi-arable land, otherwise surrounded by desert and arid plateaus, served as a sort of roadway, far safer than other approaches across unforgiving terrain, to the west. Although most likely the lands accessed by the Corridor were little known of by the Chinese at this point, in time they would grow vital. The Hexi Corridor would emerge as a frequent flashpoint.

Yet the territory gained by the nomads constituted only one part of the threat. With each victory, the Xiongnu could incorporate those subdued soldiers into their own ranks and make vassals of the vanquished, enriching themselves and funding further actions against the Han. These victories also imbued them with authority and visible momentum, which could in turn summon more tribes into the confederacy. Not only did the marriage alliance fail to forestall attacks, it also strengthened China's foe, in a way the Han would plainly discover in less than a decade.

However, Modun's letter had exaggerated somewhat. In fact, the Xiongnu had not defeated the Yuezhi, only driven the last of them from the Ordos region to Bactria (modern Afghanistan). Nonetheless, striking this blow must have been deeply meaningful for Modun, an act of retribution against the people who once made him their hostage. The timing of the campaign was ideal – perhaps a last wish? – for the *chanyu* died shortly after sending his provocative letter.

His death must have caused celebration in the Han court, for the Chinese knew the patterns of succession, how tribal groups could throw themselves into internecine conflict at a ruler's death. They surely hoped that with Modun's exit the nomadic empire, which imperfectly melded so many disparate, far-flung peoples, would fracture. Modun had been an exceptional leader, but had he built a lasting steppe empire or was he merely a lucky anomaly?

The Chinese received the answer: When Modun's son Laoshang took over as *chanyu* in 174 BC, he proved even more aggressive, wringing greater concessions in the marriage alliance than ever his father had. Among Han strategists, this must have convinced many of the need for war.

And then came 166 BC.

The Wrath of a Eunuch Spurned

Upon Laoshang's ascension, the Han court fulfilled its obligation and presented him with a princess. Accompanying her as a tutor and companion would be Zhonghang Yue, a court eunuch.

By the time of the Han, eunuchs had been a fixture in Chinese courts for more than a thousand years. Their functions ranged from serving the royal family and attending the harem – intact men were forbidden from many domains within the palace – to, over time, growing into a robust, and frequently vilified, political faction. Regular contact with the emperor and the royal family enabled them to ingratiate themselves and to learn the intricate inner workings of the empire, a position primed for corruption. Throughout Chinese history they played an outsized role in events from behind the scenes, and could pose serious threats to imperial order, as Zhonghang Yue soon did.

Ordered to the steppe for the rest of his days, he was likely surrendering a luxurious billet in a palace for a pallet in a cold tent. The embittered eunuch promised, 'My going will bring nothing but trouble to the Han!'[7] After arriving, he switched allegiances, becoming an advisor to the Xiongnu and spilling the secrets of his former masters. Versed in the ways of bureaucracy, he also advised the *chanyu* on new practices, such as running a census – this would enable the *chanyu* to tally taxes more accurately and better estimate the number of soldiers he might field in coming battles.

Zhonghang Yue also taught the Xiongnu how to counter Chinese actions. When Han envoys presented themselves to the *chanyu*, Zhonghang argued with them, in the end spitting, 'Pooh! You people in your mud huts – you talk too much! Enough of this blubbering and mouthing! Just because you wear hats, what does that make you?'[8] Committing fully to his new masters, he went on to insist that the Chinese couriers deliver only the finest goods – or else: 'Should you shortchange us after your autumn harvest, we will trample your crops with our horses'.[9] Before long, the eunuch made good on his threat, advising Laoshang to mount a massive incursion.

In the winter of 166 BC, 140,00 horsemen thundered through the passes, either unchallenged by Han soldiers or cutting their way past resistance as they stabbed into Chinese territory. Their month-long raid killed many, including the commandant of the Beidi border province, and captured people and livestock. Capitalizing on their momentum, the *chanyu* dispatched a strike force to plunge even deeper into the belly of China, burning a palace in striking distance of the capital Chang'an.

Panic flared. This was an attack like none before. A force of 1,000 chariots and 100,000 mounted troops raced to reinforce Chang'an. Fearful this could be a crippling blow to the dynasty, Emperor Jing dispatched trusted generals to take command of key garrisons, and even visited his troops and gave them gifts. He wished to take personal command of his army, ignoring his advisors' warnings against such folly. Yet, no doubt wisely, the one figure who might safely dissuade an emperor intervened first – the empress dowager, his mother.

Fitful clashes took place between the adversaries, including with a daring young horseman and archer named Li Guang, who, as we shall see in Chapter IV, later commanded huge armies in the war. Yet in a hallmark of battle with the Xiongnu – infuriating for the Chinese – once the Han army mobilized and took to the field, the enemy opted to deny them a pitched battle which might have favoured the Han. As swiftly as they had come, the Xiongnu now melted away. This was an early lesson that should the Han wish to conquer or effectively interdict the enemy, they must develop new doctrine, strategy, and tactics to do so – and amass horses so they might have a chance to contend against the vaunted Xiongnu mobility.

The decentralized structure of Xiongnu society – that tribal leaders acted independently, without the mandate or even the knowledge of the *chanyu* – could likely explain away some or even many of the earlier raids into Han. Yet one of such scale and coordination as the 166 BC incursion suggested commands flowed straight from the top. This called into question the very nature of the marriage alliance policy – if the Chinese paid such a great price in treasure and prestige, why endure these attacks? However, as their failed attempt to close with the enemy had shown, the Chinese were still not ready to meet them in battle.

Arousing Rebellion

The death of an empress dowager in 155 BC – and improperly timed carnal relations – would trigger another test for Han stability and for its tolerance of Xiongnu intrusion. Failing to observe mourning protocol of the dowager by having sex, the state of Chu's king was condemned by a court councillor – and was a capital offence. Sparing him execution, the court instead stripped Chu of one of its provinces.

The protocol violation alone was unlikely to trigger such a harsh reaction, but perhaps it was the final straw in a continuing struggle with Chu or simply a convenient pretext. To states not paying the taxes they owed to the empire, or simply straining to breathe freely under imperial control, it delivered a dire message. Learning of the punishment meted out to Chu, another Chinese kingdom, Wu, fearing a similar reduction in size, built a coalition of aggrieved states and revolted in 154 BC, setting off the Rebellion of the Seven States.

As other rebels had before, they sought and received Xiongnu support. Mounted troops stood by at the passes, ready to ride in and join the rebellion. Sensing the existential threat of a wide rebellion bolstered by Xiongnu troops, the Han snapped to action and met the separatists in battle. The Xiongnu withdrew, never joining the combat, perhaps because they forecast the rebels would not win the day. And as Modun had calculated at Baideng, his grandson, the *chanyu* Junchen (d. 126 BC), might have similarly seen that an overrun, disordered China did not serve Xiongnu purposes.

This episode highlights the complexity of managing relations between the Xiongnu and the ongoing toil, through imperial application of heat and pressure, to smelt a common 'Chinese people'. With a still fractious empire, even after more than four decades of Han rule, for some the Xiongnu still represented potential allies, a preferable partner than the imperial overlords. Indeed, it might not have been limited to an instrumental political use of the nomads. Especially in border states, some people may have felt deeper kinship with the Xiongnu than with the rarefied royals and bureaucrats of distant Chang'an.

The Han dynasty's crushing of the rebellion proved a final galvanizing action for the heretofore divided empire. For decades, significant resources had to be directed toward the central government policing its own subjects rather than dedicated to meeting external enemies. After the shock of the Rebellion of the Seven States, the empire stabilized. Kingdoms fell into line. The reigns of Wen and his son Jing focused on expanding China's agricultural base and running the state's affairs frugally; the imperial coffers swelled and accelerated a massive military build-up, each new sword forged and crossbow manufactured a step towards ending the hated marriage alliance, once a future ruler decided the time had come.

A New Kind of Emperor

In 101 BC came an imperial edict: 'From the reign of the Emperor Gaozu [Liu Bang] we have inherited the task to avenge his misfortunes at [Baideng]. Moreover, in Empress Lü's reign the court received a scandalous letter from the *chanyu*.'[10]

The edict exemplified a principal mission of the emperor Liu Che, son of Emperor Jing, here referring to his great-grandfather Liu Bang and Liu's wife. Born in 156 BC, Liu Che through good fortune and family manoeuvring was, despite not being his father's eldest son, designated crown prince in 150 BC. His father's death in 141 BC swept Liu Che to the Dragon Throne at the age of sixteen. From the outset of his reign Liu Che could look to Liu Bang's humiliation at the Battle of Baideng, the Xiongnu incursions over the decades, the threat of an alliance between the rebellious Seven Kingdoms and the Xiongnu in 154 BC, and see a need, and increasingly a mandate, to effect a radical shift in military posture. His inheritance of wealth and stability from his forefathers meant such a transformation was in reach.

Yet he did not begin this enterprise which would demand painful national sacrifice by continuing his predecessors' policies of austerity and frugality. Instead, Liu shaped a cult of personality around himself. He constructed palaces and lavish pleasure gardens, maintained a special lane in roadways for exclusive imperial use, and showcased tribute from foreign tributaries. These conspicuous displays enhanced the grandeur of the throne which perhaps, in his estimation, the empire had been lacking under the austerity of his predecessors. In a further extension of imperial might, he weakened the civil servants and councillors around him by granting more power to his corps of eunuchs, whose loyalties intensely concentrated toward him rather than to the state. All these moves laid the groundwork for effecting radical changes in the empire's direction – which civil administrators, with their own power bases and interests, might more effectively challenge.

The emperor became fixed in Chinese cosmology, a minor divinity in human guise, a lawgiver and culture-giver sanctioned by Heaven. He established new cult practices around his authority. Ritual guided much of his official duties – and he invited other influences into the court which would later carry grave consequences: as many did in that era, highborn and low, he asked shamans and soothsayers to assess various proposed actions. The *Yijing* or *Book of Changes*, a seminal text for divination, became a source he often consulted. As the Qin emperor Shi Huangdi had unsuccessfully done, the Han emperor turned to various practices and potions (likely poisonous substances such as mercury) in his quest for immortality. Yet this also made the most powerful man in China vulnerable to conmen and could trigger hysterias in the court through accusations of witchcraft. Such scandals blighted his reign, sowing chaos within the court and ultimately tampering with military operations in the field.

In 135 BC his determination to regain Chinese majesty and avenge the insults wrought by the Xiongnu came to a head. The annual marriage alliance was due for renewal – would the emperor follow decades of his forefathers' precedent, or might he risk a bolder course?

Mulling an Attack

The Xiongnu persistently reminded the court of its weakness and blemished the image of the emperor as the Son of Heaven and father of the Chinese people's collective fortunes. Further, the emperor likely imbibed the thinking that, despite rebellions and Xiongnu attacks, his dynasty had cleaved to power for six decades; with the imperial system more secure than ever before, undoubtedly, he grew eager to hack off the canker on the dynasty.

Emperor Wu of Han (156–87 BC): The 'Martial Emperor'   31

By Han reckoning, the marriage alliance system had largely backfired. The Xiongnu had prospered grandly by it, their standing and power in the region further intensified by their displacement of the Wusun and Yuezhi peoples. Rather than containing them beyond the border of the Great Wall, the Xiongnu mounted incursions and, worse, showed a continuing appetite to ally with Chinese rebels. Han ministers must have also pondered whether the Xiongnu would tire of the marriage alliance and simply mount another large-scale incursion as they had in 166 BC. Or perhaps they would simply try to sweeten their arrangements through escalating violence which would reach a point no longer endurable to the Chinese.

While intended to ensure short-term peace, the marriage alliance instead elevated the danger to China. It had, in effect, traded space, or at least the integrity of its own territory, for time, which had been spent building a mighty war machine. Though the young emperor now had to decide if this was the time to deploy it. He possessed the good sense – or political savvy – to first thoroughly explore the matter. His advisors and ministers convened to debate the merits of different possible tacks.

'The Han makes peace with the Xiongnu, but within two years they breach the agreement. Let us make no more promises, we must attack!' declared one.[11]

Yet despite the recent escalations of Xiongnu activity, the status quo held allure, as this letter to the emperor stated:

> Now, when China is not troubled by so much as the bark of a dog, to become involved in wearisome projects in distant lands that exhaust the wealth of the nation – this is hardly right for a ruler whose duty is to be a father to the people. To seek to fulfil endless ambitions, determining to win revenge and incurring the hatred of the Xiongnu – this will not bring peace to the frontier.[12]

And even were the Han to commit to a war, success or failure would be decided largely by logistics. The monstrous problem of supplying an expeditionary army traversing inhospitable terrain occupied a great deal of discussion and gradually dimmed enthusiasm for embarking on risky adventurism.

The anti-war camp could also hit a point close to home for the sovereign of a sprawling empire only recently emerging from the threat of large-scale rebellion in 154 BC:

> Today, across the land armour and swords are forged, arrows prepared and bows strung, grain is hauled, ceaselessly without rest ... Let us look to the

example of the Qin Dynasty, which fell in rebellion due to the severity of its laws and boundless appetite for war.[13]

The proximity of events with Meng Tian invading the Ordos for the Qin and the dynasty's collapse a few short years later could hardly be overlooked. Though by the same token, going to war did hold some advantages for domestic politics and social control.

When the Qin shifted from the scattered rule of feudalism to imperial domination, peasants took possession of the lands they had worked and no longer owed service to their local lords. Instead, for the Qin, and later to the Han, who adopted the practice, these peasants owed that service and taxes to the state. This squeezed the fief lords of revenues and influence, and enabled the empire to monitor and occupy its subjects. By pouring these workers into massive societal undertakings, such as civil engineering projects like digging canals and expanding the Great Wall, or laborious make-work projects, peasants could be steered away from the dangerous idleness which might blossom into rebellion. Sending young men off to war, and mobilizing society toward this enterprise, deepened this collective drive while also fostering a nationwide spirit through a common, and easily demonized, enemy.

The opposing camps on the question of going to war with the Xiongnu question roiled the court. But one pragmatist then had the last word:

> If we march thousands of miles away and try to fight with them, our men and horses will be worn out, and then the wretches will muster all their strength and fall upon us. An arrow from the most powerful crossbow, when it has reached the end of its flight, will not pierce the sheerest Lu gauze; the strongest wind, when its force is spent, will not lift a goose feather – not because both are not strong at the outset, but because their force in time is dispersed. It would not be expedient to attack the Xiongnu. Better to make peace with them![14]

That powerful metaphor carried the day, the emperor opting to renew the marriage alliance with the Xiongnu. But the days of carting off women and treasure to the north were numbered.

Liu Che Becomes The 'Martial Emperor'

Though the emperor acceded to the Xiongnu request for a new marriage alliance in 135 BC, conditions hardly improved. One general, Wang Hui, declared:

But now that there are incessant distress signals coming from our border, our soldiers and warriors are dying like flies; the hearse carts and biers are always in line of sight on the thoroughfare ... I think we should attack.[15]

The details of his thinking and of any continued debate are unknown, but it was clear from the outset that Liu Che wished to overturn the status quo of marriage alliances and free China of that embarrassing and costly encumbrance. He had wealth to burn. With his eunuchs and his cult of personality, he concentrated his power. And more voices in the court spoke together against the marriage alliance and the painful but ultimately advantageous case for war. So Emperor Liu changed his mind – or perhaps, if the renewal of the marriage alliance had only been a gambit, he chose to no longer bide his time: he would set his empire on the path to war. His steadfast commitment to a grinding war spanning the course of his long reign earned him the name by which he would be known by posterity: Emperor Wu, the 'Martial Emperor'.

Engaging the Xiongnu required determining strategy and tactics to defeat an enemy which, in many respects, the Han seemed ill suited to confront. Emperor Wu likely wanted to deliver a single decapitating blow rather than trip into a quagmire of continuous warfare, chasing the nomads across their trackless territory. Time and again, simply riding out to seek and close with the foe had failed.

A potentially instructive figure from the past was Li Mu (d. 229 BC), a general of Zhao, one of the states incorporated by the Qin which bordered Xiongnu territory, placing them in regular contact with the nomads. His strategy, defensive in the extreme, even passive, advocated that settlers flee whenever Xiongnu attacked – a policy to be so severely enforced, he suggested anyone who stood and fought face execution. Ultimately it had enabled Li Mu to snare the enemy and rout them.

Perhaps inspired by the earlier strategist, the Han general Wang Hui, gathering support for an aggressive, sharp attack, developed an approach. 'When I say attack, I do not mean penetrating deep into the heartland of our enemy. As a result of the insatiable avarice of the *chanyu* I believe we could lure him into our territories. We will select our elite troops and generals to set up an ambush and lay in wait. When he enters into the trap we will cut off his retreating path, thereupon we could capture him alive.'[16]

The war planners, headed by Wang Hui, who would take command in the field, decided not to hunt the Xiongnu in their own lands, but to gull them into a trap. It would be a low-cost stratagem insulated against catastrophic risk, including to civilian casualties – though that risk mitigation would exact a high price.

The Battle of Mayi Ushers in an Age of War

Mayi would serve as the ambush site. This was where, several decades earlier, Han Xin, a vassal king of Liu Bang, had defected to the Xiongnu. In June of 133 BC Emperor Wu ordered a Mayi man known by the Xiongnu to serve as a double agent. He went over to the enemy and declared: 'I can kill Mayi's magistrate and staff and then surrender the city to you – all its wealth will be yours.'[17] The double agent returned to the city and executed some condemned criminals, hanging their heads outside the walls and announcing to the Xiongnu: 'The officials are dead. Attack at once!'[18]

Meanwhile, 300,000 Han troops, including the skilled mounted archer Colonel Li Guang, who had helped crush the rebellion of the Seven Kingdoms, waited in ambush.

The *chanyu* Junchen swallowed the double agent's bait and with his 100,000 troops rode for Mayi. But as they moved in, the *chanyu* and his men noticed something peculiar: while the fields held livestock, no farmers tended them – the Han had prepared their ambush too well. Smelling a trap, Junchen opted to acquire some intelligence by attacking a nearby fort and capturing one of its officers, who revealed the planned operation. Swiftly the *chanyu* and his army retreated.

The Han forces gave chase but the Xiongnu enjoyed too long a lead. Even their baggage train escaped unmolested. It was an inglorious way for the Han to declare war – to hatch a decapitating ambush only for it to be detected, to reveal one's hand only to be thwarted. Someone must pay.

Wang Hui, the general who had urged the ambush, claimed that he could have attacked the baggage train, though his 30,000 soldiers would only have been cut apart by the more numerous Xiongnu, so in order to save his men, he stood down and let the foe escape.

Unfortunately for Wang, the emperor was not impressed with this reasoning:

> Wang Hui was indeed the one who engineered the Mayi plot. It was because of him that I called out several hundred thousand troops and disposed them as he recommended. Even if it was impossible to capture the shanyu, Wang Hui and his group of men could at least have attacked his baggage train and won some sort of gain to repay the soldiers for all their labour. Now if I fail to execute him, I will have no way to apologize to the empire for this failure![19]

This imperial judgement underscored the treacherous line Han generals must walk, careful to never be perceived as threatening imperial authority, and certainly to not fail in any effort in which the emperor had become so deeply invested. Similar situations occurred frequently in the coming decades of the war. In Wang Hui's case, upon learning of Emperor Wu's judgement, the general promptly committed suicide, probably hoping this quick removal from the scene might spare his family imperial ire.

Though this first Han military action failed, any illusions that a marriage alliance could keep the empires from all-out war had been dispelled. Emperor Wu cast a mammoth shadow over the ensuing decades, truly earning his title as the Martial Emperor, driving the Han to decades of struggle whose leaders – Li Guang, Wei Qing, Huo Qubing, Zhang Qian, Li Guangli, Princess Jieyou, and others – would become heroes in the Chinese annals.

Part Two

Steppe Soldiers

Chapter IV

Li Guang (d. 119 BC): The Bold and Blundering Bowman

Despite the debacle of Mayi, Emperor Wu remained committed to the warpath, though now the calculation had profoundly changed. After squandering their chance at surprise, the Han must now mount expeditions to flush or draw out the enemy – but now the Xiongnu would be in readiness. It would take several years to ramp up an offensive force, and with complex, gruelling expeditionary campaigns inevitable, the Han needed trusted, competent generals. One of those commanders, who had participated in the operation at Mayi but did not suffer Wang Hui's fate, was Li Guang, and after a famous encounter with the Xiongnu in the past, he now itched to bring the fight to them.

A Man of the Borderlands

The descendant of a renowned Qin general who hunted down a would-be assassin of Emperor Shi Huangdi, Li Guang grew up in a family of aristocratic warriors. Despite this high birth, Sima Qian, writing now about a period in which he was a firsthand witness, observed: 'I myself have seen General Li – a man so plain and unassuming that you would take him for a peasant, and almost incapable of speaking a word'.[1] In an increasingly bureaucratic military, this ineloquence would grow into an Achilles' heel.

Li grew up in Longxi, a Han commandery (one of the administrative units of the empire) in what is now the province of Gansu, China. Originating in this steppe and desert borderland made him a skilled horseman, and many great Han soldiers and generals were bred in similar frontier landscapes. Longxi was also an area contested with the Xiongnu, and the people intermingled with them, making soldiers from there familiar with, and sometimes adept at, the Xiongnu ways of war. Yet it also opened some to suspicions of their loyalties, the Han court ever vigilant against strongmen from their border provinces who could build independent power bases and establish themselves as warlords, with soldiers sworn to serve themselves, not the state. Yet few men of the empire were more capable of meeting the Xiongnu in a face-to-face clash.

In the large attack the Xiongnu made in 166 BC, a young Li Guang fought as an archer and horseman, and distinguished himself enough to secure an appointment as attendant of the imperial court. Later promoted to the imperial guards, he joined the hunting trips of Emperor Wen, who praised his warrior spirit and bemoaned, 'What a pity you were not born at a better time! Had you lived in the age of Emperor Gaozu [Liu Bang], you would have had no trouble in winning a marquisate of at least 10,000 households!'[2] Though war did come under Emperor Wu in a scale Liu Bang never faced, creating opportunity for many officers to be made wealthy nobles, this honour continually evaded Li, to his ongoing frustration.

Under Wen's son, the Emperor Jing, Li Guang earned distinction fighting as a cavalry commander against the 154 BC Rebellion of the Seven States. In a sign of political clumsiness which would increasingly cost Li, a protocol flub in the field meant that upon return to the court he earned little reward for his valour. As Sima Qian had observed, he was often tongue-tied. A more polished courtier might have finessed the infraction, but Li appeared more interested in derring-do than massaging political nuances. Perhaps Li reckoned himself of the old aristocratic mould, and his revered bloodlines appeared to discourage him from developing the nose for politics which his rivals of lesser birth had no choice but to develop. This oversight bedevilled Li throughout his career.

While in 133 BC Emperor Wu effectively declared war with the attempted Mayi ambush, low-intensity combat had been joined by Xiongnu and Han forces in the preceding decades. This gave Li Guang early exposure to the enemy. Deployed to the commandery of Shanggu along the northeast stretch of the border, he skirmished frequently and recklessly with the Xiongnu. 'Li Guang has no equal in the empire. Having the measure of his own talents, he throws himself into battle against the enemy again and again. I fear he shall soon die', reported a court official to the emperor.[3] Li's penchant for closing with the enemy, engaging his targets from twenty or thirty paces, where he could be confident of his shot, placed him in considerable danger. But this was his bombastic way and the manner of warfare in which he thrived.

Aristocratic Archery

Of Li's appearance, Sima Qian observed a 'tall man with long arms, his build made him a superb archer'.[4] The bow and arrow provided Li both with his principal weapon and primary source of diversion. He devised drinking games in which a competitor who missed his targets when shooting would be punished by swilling liquor. His powerful, long arms aided his skill – while hunting tigers (a pastime he regularly enjoyed, no matter the rank he held), he once mistook a rock for his quarry and shot, only to discover his arrow had pierced it.

Mastery of the bow ran through the generations of Li's warrior family line, and for centuries archery served as a major instrument of prestige in both military and civil spheres of China. A respected, mythologized weapon, in addition to its place on the battlefield the bow played a ceremonial role in Chinese governance and spirituality. In the Zhou dynasty (c. 1046–256 BC), aristocratic archers engaged in rites of target shooting, their accuracy but one aspect of highly choreographed, sacred movements. Notably, the original meaning of the Chinese character for 'historian' was 'the one who keeps score in a shooting contest'. Archery also ranked among the six arts of self-cultivation in ancient China, alongside music, calligraphy, ritual, mathematics, and charioteering. Confucius instructed others in the bow and used it as a metaphor for his ethical teachings: 'In archery it is not important to pierce through the leather covering of the target, since not all men have the same strength. This is the way of the ancients.'[5]

Among the pre-Han Chinese, archery with the bow remained the province of elites, not the rank and file. Composite bows were expensive to produce and challenging to operate. In some ways it harkened back to an age of heroic warfare, when warriors issued challenges to one another on the battlefield, duelling by exchanging arrows from the backs of speeding chariots. Yet, as warfare shifted from that heroic period to one of bureaucracy and attrition, archery changed. The bow demanded great strength and skill to operate, best borne out of years of training – as the Xiongnu well understood, urging their children to shoot at small animals from a young age. This long-cultivated practice could not, however, be reproduced at the scale that the state now required to carry out its war.

But with shifts in the Chinese military landscape, especially during the Warring States period (c. 475–221 BC), more peasants became involved in combat, and the vast majority lacked the background and opportunity for advanced training in archery. The advent and widespread adoption of the crossbow – the mechanized, democratized version of the composite bow – changed that. For an army swelling its ranks with peasant infantrymen, the simplicity of the crossbow over the bow meant the capacity for missile fire hugely expanded.

Chinese Military Conventions from the Earliest Days to the Han Era

Li Guang was heir to a military tradition that had changed considerably over the centuries, with the relatively recent shift in feudalism the latest shock to the goals and conduct of warfare. During the Zhou dynasty, the objective of contending polities was typically not to destroy the other but to display power and majesty, then cause the vanquished to knuckle under and offer tribute to the victors. (The Zhou were the ruling house to which the Qin served as guardians of their western flank, until the Qin came into their own.)

In the ensuing Spring and Autumn Period (770–476 BC), armies grew more professional, with the aristocratic tendencies starting to drop away. Perhaps a parallel from the ancient Mediterranean can be found in aspects of Greek warfare, its citizen-soldiers responding to the call of their small independent state, giving way to the mass organization and bureaucratic discipline of the Roman legions. In the Warring States period, the military embedded ever more deeply into everyday life. The innovation of mounted warfare further eroded the primacy of aristocratic combat and conscription became the norm. The frequency and intensity of conflict from this era can be witnessed in the scope of military texts, many of which became classics consulted across the centuries: *The Art of War*, *The Strategies of the Warring States*, and many others.

The Qin, their star rising since the days of being considered the semi-barbaric henchmen of the Zhou, prevailed over all other kingdoms in the Warring States period. The conscription which had become common practice ratcheted up, the state identifying and tracking potential soldiers like never before. As the Qin strengthened and set its ambitions toward ever greater imperial control, the objectives of armed conflict changed dramatically. Now it was not enough to subdue or cow a foe and find co-existence which simply favoured the victors, but to subjugate them utterly and ensure the defeated could not one day in the near future field an army striving for retribution. No longer did armies seek to impress their grandeur upon the adversary, but rather to unleash disciplined warfare from its gentlemanly bounds and give way to wholesale slaughter, soldiers earning cash rewards for the number of enemy heads they could tally.

The bureaucratic impulse under the Qin intensified with rising literacy levels. The concomitant centralization within the military, combined with Qin and Han infrastructure projects, such as roadbuilding and erecting the Great Wall, meant commanders in the field lost autonomy. Indeed, they carried a sort of field manual which instructed them how to respond to various battle scenarios. No doubt such fussy micromanagement flew in the face of Li Guang, a warrior of the old ways, a swaggering nobleman out to win glory, not to spin as some anonymous gear in a state war machine. Yet that was the army in which he served and commanded his troops.

The Han Soldier

Considering they served a bureaucratic regime guided by the Legalist philosophy, which believed in the inherent corruption of the individual and his debt to his state overlord, most Han conscripts and recruits probably lived under a very harsh discipline. Their training inculcated the unquestioning obedience of orders well before any consideration of imparting critical soldiering skills.

Order of Battle

The power of Han record keeping and coordination meant that it could draw troops from all quarters of its immense empire. Conscripts owed two years of service and could be reactivated in emergencies. Convicts could also earn their freedom through military enlistment, especially in desperate times.

Many soldiers assigned to the northern border remained in garrisons situated along the Great Wall. Most lacked specialized training, though some could opt for it, particularly those of higher birth. These men learned to shoot crossbows and ride horses as cavalrymen (and those posted to the coasts might become sailors). Most likely these volunteers, rather than indifferently trained conscripts, made up a sizeable element of expeditionary forces striking at the Xiongnu.

Units of five men formed a *wu*, the smallest cell of the army. The number five was an auspicious one, associated with the *wuxing*, the 'five phases of matter' which constituted the universe in Chinese reckoning. Two *wu* units combined to form a grouping of ten, named a *zu* (these numbers also correspond to Legalist organizations of society, in which groups of five and ten subjects supported and monitored each other). From these units they expanded into larger variations, such as the *hou* or platoon, five of which constituted a *hou guan* or company.[6]

Duty at the Garrisons

Little is known of combat troops' field experiences against the Xiongnu. Those troops garrisoned at the border often manned watchtowers, which were arranged so that two could be in sight of each other. At a sign of trouble, they would ignite their ready-made fires, the smoke sending the warning by day, and an element added to the fire producing a white smoke visible by night. They also used a semaphore system, signalling to other fortifications along the Wall with flags. A break in the regular contact between towers indicated that the defences had been compromised. Sentries along the Wall and at the passes also controlled the outflow of Chinese into the steppe.

Arms and Armour

For its time, Han China boasted a considerable industrial capacity and sophisticated metallurgy. As a result of this, Chinese soldiers wore excellent armour. Many donned suits of lamellar, its sturdy scales, set in a structure of hardened leather, sometimes numbering in the hundreds. Soldiers could carry high-quality swords, spears, halberds or axes into battle. China could also manufacture the trigger mechanisms for crossbows on a huge scale, and this weapon provided the Chinese with most of their missile fire. A weapon outmatching the composite bow in power, the crossbow had a range of perhaps 150 metres. Archers fighting with bows rather than crossbows were likely considered more specialized marksmen.

One weapon system they employed, its uses still not well understood, was the chariot. The introduction of the Chinese chariot remains murky; most likely it rolled in from the Russian steppe in the second millennium BC. The mystery around the vehicle extends to its precise military applications. Certainly some models transported officers about the battlefield, supporting command and control, some of which held towers from which observers had vantage over the battlefield. For combat models, the likeliest function was as mobile archery platforms, with one or two bowmen plying arrows into the enemy; spearmen and scythed axles warded off swarming attacks by infantry.

A war chariot barrelling at an infantryman certainly made for a terrifying sight, yet the weapon system's shortcomings were plain. To operate they required a suitable space free of pitfalls and broken ground. In the expeditionary context of seeking contact with Xiongnu, a Han force straying ever farther from their overstretched supply lines, those shortcomings only intensified. Nonetheless, for reasons of ingrained military culture, or because they offered some battlefield utility unknown to modernity, chariots remained a part of the Han arsenal and mainstays of expeditionary campaigns like those Li Guangli commanded.

A Soldier's General

Though in some ways a remote noble, Li also cultivated a strong bond with his men. In the field he ate the same rations as his soldiers and endured the same harsh conditions, forgoing the perquisites of his rank. His was a loose, flexible style, and rather than behaving like some military martinet, he gave his men much freedom to do as they thought best, such as the manner in which they established camps while on campaign. The combination of a decentralized command style, his personal touch with his men, and the bold example he gave through personal risk earned him the lasting admiration of his soldiers.

His preference for flexibility and speed over rigidity and regulations contributed to a talent for fighting Xiongnu – so much so that he came to be known by them as the 'Flying General'. An acclaimed incident in 144 BC showed how he earned this moniker. While Li was stationed at a fort set along the northern border, the site of recent Xiongnu raids, a eunuch army officer posted there went out riding with a band of horsemen and spied three Xiongnu hunters. Outnumbering them, the eunuch officer and his men attacked, but the Xiongnu kept their distance and picked off the bulk of the band. Barely escaping, the eunuch made it back and reported in. Li and one hundred of his men raced out, slaying two of the hunters and capturing the third.

Then Li noticed thousands of armed Xiongnu gathered, watching him. The three hunters must have been scouts or perhaps decoys deliberately tasked with baiting the Chinese out into the open. Li's soldiers pressed for a rapid retreat to their base. But he quickly conjured a different plan.

> Since our army lies ten or fifteen miles away, if we attempt to race back the Xiongnu will be at our heels, shooting at us all the while. Better to remain here and make them believe we are meant to lure them into an attack by our army.[7]

Indeed, even this proved too tame for his tastes, soon ordering his men to advance closer to the enemy. He then commanded they dismount and remove their saddles, explaining that this brazen display would make the deception even more convincing.

On a white horse a lone Xiongnu commander ventured out for a closer look, but Li shot him from his mount. Baffled by the display of sang-froid, the Xiongnu force came to believe an ambush was in the offing, and eventually they melted away. Li's brazen bluff, which surely saved his life and those of his men, was a ploy the Xiongnu, whose warfare often depended on cunning ruses, might have themselves put to use.

The First Expeditionary Campaigns

Several years passed after the abortive Mayi ambush until the empire readied itself for assaults of Xiongnu territory. The objectives of the first campaign, in 129 BC, were to seize lands in the Ordos, specifically that vital conduit to the west, the Hexi Corridor. Among other advantages, this would gain the Han land for raising horses and deny the same to the Xiongnu. Four generals, including Li, each leading a force of 10,000, set out in an attempt to surprise the Xiongnu looking to trade at marketplaces situated along the border. The columns moved separately, likely to cover greater swathes of territory. Li and his cavalry departed from Yanmen ('Wild Goose Gate'), a vital mountain pass at the mouth of the steppe.

The launch of this massive campaign at first held great promise for Li. Serving as a colonel of the imperial guard, he received a temporary promotion to the rank of general. Under the Han, a commander did not typically hold general's rank as a standing position – the equivalent of colonel was in nearly all instances the highest – but only for particular campaigns. Still, this was a great achievement for Li, one step closer to rising to the marquisate, just as Emperor Wu's father, Emperor Wen, had mentioned on the hunt.

But the campaign broke quite the other way for Li. His rival Wei Qing, commanding one of the other columns, later earned commendation for his performance, as we will see in Chapter VI. But Li's campaign inaugurated a string of misfortunes which would jeopardize Li's career going forward.

It all began after Li encountered a Xiongnu force greatly outnumbering his and the fighting turned desperate. Perhaps he dropped many foes with flawless bow shots, devised ruses and inspired his men to great acts of bravery – but the outcome was inevitable: the massacre of Li's unit. With his reputation as the 'Flying General' known to the Xiongnu, the *chanyu* Junchen directed his men to take Li alive if possible and bring the Chinese general before him. After Li took a wound, some Xiongnu found him and prepared to fulfil their *chanyu*'s wish. His captors laid the general, apparently so badly injured as to be unresponsive, on a stretcher made of ropes lashed between a pair of horses and rode off.

However, General Li's wounds were not as grave as they appeared, nor had his guile left him. As he lay on the stretcher feigning incapacity, he eyed a boy to his side riding a powerful horse. Without warning he sprang from the stretcher onto the horse's back, seized the boy's bow, shoved him to the ground, and galloped off. With this captured bow he dissuaded the pursuers, and eventually he caught up with the remnants of his defeated army limping back to China.

Though he made a daring escape, thoughts of what manner of imperial judgement he would face must have weighed heavily on Li. After all, Wang Hui, the general of the failed Mayi ambush, took his own life before he could be executed – and had not even lost any men in that mishap. Li Guang had sacrificed many – in vain – and also allowed himself to be captured. Might the same fate await him?

The Price of Failure

To serve the Han at its highest levels brought a life of privilege, the chance at wealth and social standing, yet prominence before the emperor also made one an easy target. When Li dragged himself back to the capital, it appeared his valiant efforts to escape the Xiongnu only delayed a death sentence. Emperor Wu ordered Li's arrest for his failure and made the following pronouncement:

> [In accordance with] the laws governing the use of troops, failure in being diligent or in instructing [the troops] is the fault of a general or a leader; [whereas] when instructions and orders have been proclaimed clearly, not to be able to use all his power [in obeying those instructions and orders] is the crime of an officer or a soldier. [These] generals have already been given into the charge of the Commandant of Justice, who is to apply the law and execute them.[8]

In the end, the Commandant of Justice opted to spare Li's life, but he did not escape punishment. For his crime, Li paid an onerous fine and was reduced to commoner status. This time, he evaded the worst excesses of Han justice.

Humiliated, Li went into retirement. An irascible side to him now emerged, perhaps heightened by his demotion and near-execution. While on a hunting trip, he ventured past a guarded gatehouse and on his return, drunk, he was ordered to halt and challenged by a sentry. Unmoved by Li's protestations of his former general rank, the soldier pointed out that Li had violated the curfew in effect at night. Eventually Li bullied his way through the gateway, but not without remembering that soldier who had questioned him. In some ways, their exchange reflected in microcosm a broader clash of a colossal, rulebound bureaucracy with an individual who traded on swagger and glamour.

Emperor Wu, his anger at Li Guang's capture and poor performance in the field apparently fading, reinstated Li into his good graces and appointed him governor of the northeastern commandery of Youbeiping. Li's fearsome reputation apparently discouraged attacks in that region, for he barely encountered the Xiongnu. But Li turned to another perceived enemy and in doing so revealed his vengeful character. Restored to high military authority, Li ordered the watchman who had challenged him brought under his command and promptly repaid that dutiful soldier by executing him.

It was an ignominious act, all the more so from one so celebrated as a soldier's general and a man beloved by his troops. Li even apologized to Emperor Wu for his rashness but the emperor saw no reason for remorse, pointing out the benefit of being perceived as merciless.

More Lacklustre Campaigning

In parallel with Wei Qing, a supreme commander with whom he would later lock horns, in 123 BC Li conducted a search-and-destroy mission; still his poor luck endured, and he returned to the capital without notching up a single enemy engagement. Perhaps this time the Xiongnu opted to deny battle with the feared 'Flying General', Li now becoming a victim of his reputation built on prior successes. Or possibly, in the stupefying vastness of the steppes and deserts, the two enemies simply failed to stumble onto one another.

In 121 or 120 BC, Li commanded 4,000 cavalrymen on campaign, this time accompanied by his son Li Gan. They rode out with another unit of 10,000 cavalry, commanded by Zhang Qian, an explorer, diplomat and general who played a major part in China's expansion into Central Asia, the nascent Silk Road, and the Han-Xiongnu War (his story is told in Chapter VIII). The two units split, Li's force advancing deep into Xiongnu territory, only to fall into a trap laid by the Sage King of the Left. Commanding 40,000 horsemen, he surrounded Li and his cavalry. No matter how skilled Li might be as a horseman and Xiongnu-fighter, being outnumbered 10 to 1 imposed a merciless arithmetic. And General Zhang Qian and his 10,000 men were nowhere to be seen.

Yet in a past crisis Li had intimidated an entire Xiongnu army with a tiny detachment of soldiers. Perhaps reading the fear in his men and recognizing a courageous display might ginger them up, he commanded his son, along with twenty or thirty other horsemen, to sally out and charge the enemy. It appeared to surprise the Xiongnu, the Han cavalry scattering them. When Li Gan returned, he declared, 'Collecting the ears of dead barbarians is easy work!', lifting the men's spirits.[9] In that action Li Gan proved he was of the same bold stock as his father – something which in a few short years brought the young man to his doom.

With a symbolic blow struck against the Xiongnu, and perhaps showing his soldiers that those mounted demons were merely men, Li Guang began turning the situation around. He would need cover if they hoped to survive this battle, but suitable natural features were in short supply in this region. So he ordered his soldiers to position the wagons of their baggage train into a ring, then used that as an improvised defensive feature (this tactic would reappear shortly in a seminal battle with the Xiongnu).

The enemy galloped around the barricade, deluging arrow volleys and killing many Han troops. General Li ordered his men to ready their crossbows, yet to hold their shots. With his own crossbow – nicknamed 'Big Yellow'– he targeted enemy leaders, including the Xiongnu second-in-command, demoralizing

Li Guang (d. 119 BC): The Bold and Blundering Bowman   49

and driving them back. When the Xiongnu attack ebbed, Li tried to hearten his men by chatting and joking with them as he adjusted their formations, knowing on the next day they would face more devastating assaults, and they could simply not endure many more of those. Only by holding fast could they possibly survive. And only by a relief force riding in could they possibly escape. Where was fellow general Zhang Qian and his 10,000 cavalry?

The Han army had a zeal for attempting complicated linkups in the featureless regions of the Xiongnu. It would play tragic and sometimes comic parts throughout the war, bringing generals into danger of humiliation, reduction in rank, and execution, as both Zhang Qian and Li Guang learned.

Fighting raged into the following day. Li and his men held out, though more than half the survivors of the previous day's battle now fell. At last their tenacity was rewarded – in thundered Zhang Qian with his 10,000 soldiers and the Xiongnu beat a retreat.

Perhaps Li speculated about what imperial judgement might await him this time. The engagement had not been nearly as disastrous as his previous battle with the Xiongnu, but he had again failed to subdue the enemy. Even so, upon returning to China he avoided criminal charges and retained his command. Maybe he could win a marquis title yet.

For this stubborn failure rankled him, as Li even visited a soothsayer, named Wang Shuo, to discuss the matter. The combination of his chronic poor luck, his lack of supporters within the court, and an apparent distaste for politicking stymied his advancement. Men of lesser ability and stature, even some among his own subordinates, had already been ennobled as marquises.

> Ever since the Han started attacking the Xiongnu, I have never failed to be in the fight. I've had men in my command who were company commanders or even lower and who didn't even have the ability of average men, and yet twenty or thirty of them have won marquisates on the strength of their achievements in attacking the barbarian armies. I have never been behind anyone else in doing my duty. Why is it I have never won an ounce of distinction so that I could be enfeoffed like the others?[10]

The diviner asked him to search his past for regrettable actions.

> 'Once,' answered Li, 'when I was governor of Longxi, the Qiang tribes in the west [a people of the Tibetan Plateau] started a revolt. I tried to talk them into surrendering, and in fact persuaded over 800 of them to give themselves up. But then I went back on my word and killed them all the very same day. I have never ceased to regret what I did.

'Nothing brings greater misfortune than killing those who have already surrendered to you,' said Wang Shuo. 'This is the reason, general, that you have never become a marquis!'[11]

Shifting from the cosmic to the dirt of realpolitik, perhaps too, Li's background as a subject from the frontier and the loyalty he inspired among his men might have inspired paranoia in the emperor. As someone who had already run afoul of imperial expectations but been allowed to keep his life, maybe Emperor Wu and his advisors questioned whether the old man had been embittered by his former reduction to commoner rank. The emperor's forebears had fended off and thwarted numerous rebellions, often sparking near the border with the Xiongnu. Popular with his men, Li possessed the wherewithal to position himself as a warlord. His indifference to politics, or at least insensitivity to its currents, might have given rise to a perception he was more challenging to control, or at least unpredictable. Regardless of the level of suspicion directed at him, the court's patience with Li's middling performance began to wear thin, and his future hinged on the outcome of his next campaign.

Death in the Desert

The campaign of 119 BC into the Northern Desert (the Gobi), intended to traverse huge distances through punishing conditions to attack the *chanyu* and his army. The plan probably gave the general pause well before he set out as it involved another complicated in-field rendezvous despite the limited communications over huge distances. This time, instead of with Zhang Qian, Li would link with an army led by the supreme commander Wei Qing, with whom Li had first campaigned in 129 BC. By now Li was an old man, and even for a general in the bloom of youth these manoeuvres in the field must have tested stamina and skill.

Yet forces behind the scenes already acted against him. While Emperor Wu would excuse his brashness in killing a sentry too diligent with his work and the loss of nearly his entire unit, he was not as quick to ignore the ill luck which dogged General Li. For this campaign, the emperor directed Wei Qing that Li should not be entrusted with a major role. 'He is not to pursue the *chanyu*', he told Wei Qing. Despite his protests, Li was shifted away from the vanguard position he had been planning on and told instead to follow a long and complicated route to the junction point.[12]

The Han army crossed the desert and in its northern extremity, joined battle with the Xiongnu. It was hard fought and proved to be a turning point for the Han – but General Li was not there. Running late and becoming lost in the featureless terrain, he missed both the rendezvous with Wei Qing and the whole of the battle.

At last he arrived. Wei Qing sent a clerk to upbraid Li and summon him to answer for his crimes. Li insisted that the fault lay entirely with him, not any of his men, and that he would report later to Wei. The general then called together his officers and said to them,

> Since I was old enough to wear my hair bound up, I have fought over seventy engagements, large and small, with the Xiongnu. This time I was fortunate enough to join the general in chief in a campaign against the soldiers of the *Shanyu* himself, but he shifted me to another division and sent me riding around by the long way. On top of that, I lost my way. Heaven must have planned it this way![13]

His path had run its course. A brilliant turn in this battle might have corrected his trajectory and earned him a marquisate, or at least recognition by Emperor Wu as a leader of some competence once again. 'Now I am over sixty – much too old to stand up to a bunch of petty clerks and their charges!' Li added to his men.[14]

And at that, with his sword the luckless general killed himself.

Over the course of his decades-long career, the Xiongnu never cowed him, but the bureaucracy did. Sima Qian wrote that at his death 'the men of the army and the common people wept without cease, such was their admiration for the general'.[15] And for his son Li Gan, grief mingled with reckless anger, which to his ultimate regret, soon he would attempt to satisfy.

Chapter V

Chanyu Yizhixie (d. 114 BC): Leader of an Embattled Empire

Except for the ephemeral Qin dynasty, until Emperor Wu's tenure the Xiongnu had little exposure to a consolidated Chinese enemy. From the time of Modun's recapture of the Ordos and through the ensuing six decades, the nomads had launched repeated incursions into Chinese territory and surely also repelled encroachments which were launched by Chinese border states. Despite frequent violations, the marriage alliance poured growing rewards on the Xiongnu Empire. By lending occasional support to Chinese rebels, the nomads helped keep the Han so preoccupied with maintaining its own integrity that military solutions against the nomads became untenable. So ran the thinking of the Xiongnu. Yet warning signs gathered that China was mobilizing on a scale not seen since the previous century.

In 139 or 138 BC the Xiongnu discovered a secret diplomatic mission by the Han seeking nomadic allies, led by the emissary Zhang Qian (who later rescued Li Guang from encirclement by a Xiongnu army). This put the Xiongnu on alert of escalating Chinese attempts to break the status quo under the marriage alliance and gird for war. Then in 133 BC came the attempted ambush at Mayi, the Xiongnu narrowly avoiding that which might have ravaged their military capacity for a generation. And yet it is likely they did not believe there would be sustained appetite for war. The *chanyu* Junchen, whose reign from 160 BC until his death in 126 BC rivalled his grandfather Modun's in duration, perhaps dismissed the abortive Mayi ambush as the brash action of a young, untested Han emperor, and believed the Chinese had learned their lesson after attempting to draw the vaunted Xiongnu into an ambush.

But then came the campaigns of 129 BC commanded by Li Guang, Wei Qing, and others. In 127 BC the Han, after seizing lands around the Yellow River's bend, rebuilt and reoccupied Qin walls and forts. The Xiongnu, perhaps expecting China's combat performance to track closer to Liu Bang's Battle of Baideng in 200 BC, instead found themselves on the back foot. The Han proved both durable and aggressive; even if they sometimes annihilated Han units, the Xiongnu must have understood they were now locked in a fight with an adversary prepared to shoulder tremendous losses in lives and treasure to win.

What motivated Xiongnu aggression? Especially as the war wore on, the nomads might be considered more a desperate than a rapacious force. They fought not only for unchallenged control of the steppe and other lands outside of China, but for raw survival. Their pastoral way of life carried inherent dangers. Even in times when Han expeditionary forces did not invade and pillage their lands, a nasty winter or poor pasturage growth could bring famine. Han seizures of herds – in 127 BC alone they stole a million head of livestock – could intensify this vulnerability to a horrifying degree. With such a meagre population, the Xiongnu simply could not well absorb losses to hunger on top of those killed in battle.

Far from the days of Modun at the Battle of Baideng, when in their hands the Xiongnu held the fate of the Han, now the nomads stood in great jeopardy. To ward off starvation and to defend their violated lands, they needed a leader to put forward an effective strategy and galvanize them into an enemy which could convince the Chinese to revert to the status quo.

Facing Foes Within and Without

At Junchen's death in the winter of 126 BC, a power struggle broke out for the throne. On one side conspired his son Yudan (sometimes written as Yuchan), whose scrabble for the *chanyu* title violated the standard mode of succession. Junchen's younger brother Yizhixie, the rightful heir by Xiongnu custom, contested his nephew's claim.

Little is known of Yizhixie's early life. As the brother of the *chanyu*, he likely rode with Junchen toward Mayi and withdrew with all the others after detecting the ambush; at the least he would have been intimately familiar with its details and perhaps weighed in with the *chanyu*'s council on its implications. Further, through formal instruction or long observation he would have learned the methods of administering the complicated confederacy and the making of war, as Yudan found out when the struggle for the throne gave way to violence. Older and more experienced, Yizhixie quickly prevailed in a decisive battle.

Despite the succession resolving without protracted turmoil, such messy transfers of power must have eroded the already weak imperial culture of the Xiongnu. Yet who in the empire could overlook the fact that the newly strengthened Xiongnu Empire had taken to its feet through the coup and assassination carried out by Yizhixie's grandfather Modun against his own father? So long as the new *chanyu* demonstrated wise judgement and a cool head, and delivered security and wealth, much could be forgiven. At this time, however, any *chanyu* faced unprecedented challenges to delivering such goods to his people.

After his defeat, Yudan managed to escape Yizhixie with his life, retreating into the waiting arms of the Han. No doubt the Chinese revelled in welcoming a Xiongnu prince into their fold. This set a dangerous example to other Xiongnu, demonstrating that breaking from the confederacy and going over to the enemy could earn rewards (in due course this happened again, but with far more catastrophic effects on the nomadic empire). The alliance provided the foundation for Xiongnu subordinates, inspired by greed or because they had fallen into disfavour with their *chanyu*, to find a lifeline in the Han by defecting to them.

With Yudan no longer posing a threat and his claim to the title firm, Yizhixie now had to find a way to govern the Xiongnu and counter a foe whose resources dwarfed his own.

Directing a War While Governing an Empire

As *chanyu*, Yizhixie began each day bowing to the sun, at night to the moon. The Xiongnu sought counsel from these heavenly bodies and Tengri, and it is likely that all the challenges of organizing a disunited mass constantly preyed on his mind. Leading a multilingual, multi-ethnic confederacy with no underlying religious dogma, a loose political doctrine, and limited collective vision based around mutual survival would test the limits of every *chanyu*'s leadership talents – the trading, intimidation, courting, and payoffs necessary to unite varied efforts and indeed, to simply hold the confederacy together. It must have demanded incredible energy to coordinate among the willing and pre-empt those who might waver in their allegiance to the empire, especially over an enormous swathe of land encompassing steppe, mountains and deserts, all at the speed of a horse. All this proved a decided disadvantage against a foe who could organize better than almost any people in the world at that time, who all the while was marshalling more power and seeking to drive wedges into Xiongnu unity by offering private arrangements with defectors like Yudan.

Plotting Strategy at the Autumn Assemblies

Autumn, as the winds gathered pace across the open spaces of Central Asia, heralded the period when the Xiongnu stood most united. Annual assemblies took place at the *chanyu*'s court, with kings and tribal leaders from across the vast empire reporting in. Hunts, games such as horse racing and horse-jumping competitions, and other festivities diverted the representatives and encouraged bonds among far-flung peoples. Taxes were collected, disputes heard and resolved, and other routine matters of governance addressed. After Yizhixie came to power, surely one topic dominated discussion: the war effort against the Han.

Winter was an especially dangerous season for nomadic pastoralists, when frosts could destroy pasturage and thin their herds, or cold snaps kill livestock where they stood. Chinese crops, on the other hand, would have been freshly harvested and packed in granaries, allowing for Xiongnu raids to garner vital foodstuffs, captives, and other wealth. Thus autumn proved the ideal season to plan raids and other military actions.

The assembly having resolved to fight, the task fell to Yizhixie, his junior kings, and other leaders to determine how best to confront such a massive, organized, and ever-emboldened enemy. The Han presented a profoundly different opponent from the Yuezhi, the Donghu and other steppe peoples they had faced – all tribal forces who were similarly constrained as the Xiongnu themselves in numbers. Not so the Chinese whose ability to tap an almost bottomless well of men meant, if the Xiongnu assessed their prospects in a purely rational light, that if the war were conducted through nothing but a series of pitched battles, the Han would assuredly claim victory. No matter that the individual Xiongnu warrior probably far outclassed the typical Han soldier.

They required a vision to give purpose to their force of arms. The strategic goals of Yizhixie were to preserve the sanctity of Xiongnu lands and keep tributaries from other regions firmly within their orbit. Binding their fate with the Han through marriage alliance proved the essential means to achieve this. A variety of methods could be brought to bear, but all effectively conformed to a guerilla strategy, though enacted at the scale of an empire to frighten the Chinese, drain their resources, and sap their military and political will. The Xiongnu surely realized what high expenses and dangerous, unpopular campaigns against them would incur for the Han, so provoking the powerful but lumbering empire to continue mounting expeditions to the point of utter exhaustion appeared a cunning stance.

The Marriage Alliance and Its Strategic Imperatives

Total victory over China was neither practicable nor preferable. This unusual military objective emerged out of Modun's superior position over the early Han at Baideng, when he could have destroyed the nascent empire in one fell swoop. Instead, in Baideng's aftermath Modun struck a bargain with China which ensured Xiongnu territorial integrity while also building up strength and, in turn, bleeding Chinese resources and thus weakening them. Over time, the alliance further sweetened, with Modun's son Chanyu Laoshang extracting greater wealth out of the Chinese through the severity of his threats.

A view of lazy, parasitic nomads preying on the wealth of the Chinese, backing up their demands with violence can easily take shape, but this fails to recognize the 'defensive' features of the marriage alliance for the Xiongnu. They wished to exploit the treaty to husband their strength, for, as they were, by interest or necessity, players in Chinese politics, they likely held intelligence, or could simply surmise, that China dreamed of the day it would again go on the offensive against them. Just as the Qin had invaded, so too would the Han once its house stood in order. For decades the treaties had kept the Chinese out of Xiongnu lands, and while they had to pay eyewatering sums and suffer the indignity of sending off Chinese women as brides, the Chinese did not take terrible battle casualties. And until Emperor Wu sat on the throne, this made for a compelling argument.

The marriage alliance was a well offering sweet water which seemed never to run dry, though poison slowly seeped in through the underlying soil. While valuable, the alliance also warped Xiongnu development. The constant resort to China and the marriage alliance stunted new opportunities, such as venturing even further west to conquer new lands and establish vassalages. On the one hand Chinese payouts enabled Yizhixie and other Xiongnu elites to reward their followers, who in turn passed down some of that wealth to their own men. Yet on the other, those who felt insufficiently rewarded would simply ignore the peace with China and launch raids to gather their own plunder, not only diminishing overall Xiongnu military coordination but tainting the *chanyu* in the eyes of the Chinese, exposing his lack of central authority.

Yizhixie thus enjoyed little freedom in his choices. To appease his subordinate leaders who came to him with their hands out for largesse and to stave off Han incursions, Yizhixie had to pursue a strategy which, with the proper application of pressure, would convince the Chinese to see wisdom in restoring the marriage alliance. This pressure depended on military power. What resources and tactics could he bring to bear? And what weaknesses militated against him?

A Warrior Society

The Xiongnu military structure, culture, and capabilities radically differed from those of the Han. As herdsmen, hunters, and warriors, these nomads, trained in archery and horsemanship from a tender age, their environment one which instilled toughness, battle-hardened through frequent intertribal clashes, under certain conditions thrived in warfare. Hunting accorded with their way of war based on speed, mobility, scouting, and the identification and exploitation of vulnerabilities. At first blush it appears the Xiongnu would make an unstoppable army. Yet the manner of their combat, however devastating in suitable contexts, did not always align with the strategic realities of defeating a highly organized opponent.

Unlike the Han, whose emperor commanded by fiat, the *chanyu* and other leaders coaxed and persuaded their troops into action. It is likely that Xiongnu warriors were less concerned with discipline and deference to commanders and, perhaps, not as vulnerable to harsh punishment for disobedience and failure as were their Han counterparts, whose questioning or refusal to serve would risk grave punishment.

While China surely represented a widely understood threat, economic interests frequently motivated military activity for the Xiongnu. A successful raid or subjugation of a rival tribe snatched personal enrichment in the form of plunder, access to new pastures, and slaves. 'In the aftermath of a battle, warriors who could show the enemy heads they collected received a cup of liquor, plundered their slain foes, and made slaves of their captives.'[1] Thus individual motivations fired Xiongnu soldiers, not simply decrees from their leadership. At the tactical level, individual drives must have fragmented coordinated actions on the battlefield, with soldiers striving for personal enrichment at the cost of tactical cohesion. Yet perhaps their decentralized command structure obviated this, with Xiongnu soldiers better able to act on their own initiative. And, certainly, their renowned manoeuvrability compensated for much of the potential weakness arising from disorderly battlefield actions.

Doctrine

The greatest combat advantage the Xiongnu enjoyed, and a fundamental aspect of their nature as a civilization, was their mobility. Practically born to the saddle, their command of horsemanship meant they could often instigate, avoid, or withdraw from battle, especially when fighting an enemy as footbound and chronically short on horses as the Han. Conquering land and then defending it from recapture neither made sense as a strategic aim nor did it cohere with Xiongnu cultural drives or the cycles of sustaining their herds. With no baggage train per se, as their provisions were their sheep and other herd animals, highly mobile until going under the slaughtering knife, the logistics which would bog down Han forces barely signified for the Xiongnu.

Their doctrine perhaps means the Xiongnu are best seen as a large-scale guerilla or insurgency force. They excelled at low-intensity warfare, the sort of actions they routinely practised on their tribal enemies, primarily through raids. They could apply violence in the proper measure to achieve a policy aim, broadly their desire to either strengthen the marriage alliance in the period before Mayi, or restore it after de facto war had broken out. Modun's decision at the Battle of Baideng to allow the Han to retreat exemplified that canny use of moderated violence over a yearning for total conquest.

Tactics and Capabilities

The tactical options available to the Xiongnu derived principally from their doctrine and war culture. To the disgust of the Chinese, unless hemmed in and forced to fight, the horsemen only committed to battle as it favoured them: 'They advance when to their benefit; when to their disadvantage, they retreat, and feel not the least bit of shame about this'.[2]

Masterful horsemanship and mobility granted a huge advantage in their use of scouting. This enabled them to lead the Chinese into traps and ambushes, and, unless surprised, to choose the battleground which best served. Undoubtedly this delivered them from annihilation when slipping out of the trap at Mayi in 133 BC. Furthermore, in contrast to the Chinese expeditions straying far from their bases, operating in their own lands enhanced scouting capabilities.

As a small and nimble force contending against a numerically superior but unwieldy one, their high speed, which enabled them to attempt breaches of Han defences in one location only to break off and probe another, compelled the Han to commit men over enormous areas. This meant the Xiongnu could wear down their opponent and easily prevent concentration of their resources.

In a mainstay of steppe warfare, they also excelled at luring their enemies far from their main bodies of support. Often they employed a feigned retreat, in which an overzealous foe, convinced they verged on achieving a rout, chased their supposedly fleeing enemy to a trap. The Han had learned this lesson at great cost when Modun cunningly strung out Liu Bang's forces in the Battle of Baideng and encircled him.

In addition to employing such ruses as the feigned retreat, Xiongnu also exploited the often grey, ambiguous relations with the Han, in which some were believed friendly to Chinese interests. In one instance a Xiongnu, considered a reliable informant, reported to a Chinese commander that the main Xiongnu force was nowhere near. In light of this the commander received permission to grant the bulk of his soldiers leave to return to their farms. Shortly thereafter, the Xiongnu returned *en masse* and laid waste to the region.

That contact between Chinese and Xiongnu also promoted the Xiongnu to incorporate defectors in their ranks. With disaffected Chinese soldiers and officers facing grim punishments for failure (such as Li Guang being hounded to the point of suicide) and serving a system which might offer little personal reward to them, the Xiongnu, who did not insist newcomers obey a particular ideology or dogma, were able to entice their opponents to join the Xiongnu ranks. With many Han soldiers and officers hailing from the northern border regions – their familiarity with the Xiongnu making them the most effective fighting men – no doubt this background eased the recruitment process.

Raids

Perhaps the best expression of their mobile warfare, what became a hallmark tactic and key to pursuing Xiongnu strategic goals, was the raid. They could be finely calibrated, from the simple plundering of a farm to the sack of a frontier settlement, according to the objective. It accords with the Xiongnu desire to use warfare as a controlled policy instrument, one which could prick the Han to drive them back to the bargaining table to confirm or improve the terms of a *chanyu*'s marriage alliance with the Chinese state.

For training and maintaining combat fitness, the raid, along with hunting, also kept warriors poised for larger-scale operations. In addition, they raked more Chinese wealth into Xiongnu coffers, potentially funding more substantial campaigns down the line. Raids thus achieved numerous ends without a full-blown committal of forces to sustained combat.

However, because the raid could be effected in a decentralized fashion, it must be noted that often they did not take the form of strategic, top-level Xiongnu government action, but rather the actions of opportunists striking out independently for riches and glory. Raids must have had complex motives, varying often, though such subtleties were not recorded or even likely recognized by most Chinese chroniclers. And it must be remembered small-scale attacks ascribed to the 'Xiongnu' by Chinese might have been carried out by tribesmen who barely identified with that empire and did not receive clearance from higher authorities to mount an attack.

Order of Battle

While the Xiongnu brought together scores of tribes under the power of a single *chanyu*, nonetheless their comparatively low troop strength plagued them. This made it difficult to absorb losses, while the Chinese could draw from a seemingly inexhaustible supply of manpower, through conscription, corvée service, converting convicts into soldiers, and other means. Though the Xiongnu lacked numbers, they could field a greater proportion of their people, drawing soldiers from across society. Their children could serve as fighters, for they trained in archery, hunting, and probably other military activities from a young age.

Based on findings at gravesites which reveal skeletons showing marks of combat injuries and weapons as prominent burial goods, it is likely women, at least in some circumstances, joined the army ranks. As a nomadic society in which raids were frequent and unexpected, mobilizing all possible military strength, drawing from anyone fit to fight, would have been critical to a tribe's survival. The style of Xiongnu combat widened the spaces for women to be effective: riding on horseback and shooting bows (albeit bows which demanded tremendous strength to draw) both levelled the battlefield for women who sought to take up arms against their enemies.

Weaponry

The Xiongnu wielded swords, maces, spears and axes, yet the steppe composite bow was their trademark and the weapon which placed Han soldiers in the greatest peril.

Construction of these sophisticated weapons was painstaking and expensive. Through the curing of materials, binding of wood and horn to form the body, the making of animal glue, the stringing of the bow with silken cord or sinew, the fletching of arrows with eagle feathers, the production of these weapons could span several months.

The Xiongnu steppe bow likely had an effective range of 175 metres (500 feet), with expert archers confidently accurate at ranges of 50 to 60 metres (160 to 200 feet). The range and power of Chinese crossbows outclassed the bow, yet the simple, clumsy crossbow was ill-suited to the Xiongnu way of highly mobile warfare; the crossbow belonged to a different culture and mentality. Xiongnu had access to crossbows – by capturing them or through manufacture, as they had the necessary fabrication skills and material – but rejected them as inferior to their native weapon.

Terrain

The harsh landscape of the Xiongnu perhaps served as their most damaging weapon against the Han and a key element in their strategy. With territory encompassing forest, steppe, desert, mountains, and other rugged topographical elements, this terrain could be inimical to life for those not born to it, who hadn't been raised with a range of cultural adaptations, such as pastoralism, to survive there. In effect, the Xiongnu could use their homeland as a sturdy shield against Han aggression, and a deadly trap for those daring to breach it. With storms and extreme temperature ranges from searing heat to cold which could inflict frostbite or worse – the landscape itself seemed to lie in ambush for invaders.

The Xiongnu subsisted primarily on their herds, which travelled with them. For the Chinese, throughout all their expeditionary campaigns in the north, logistics remained the supreme challenge, especially for larger forces. Swollen Chinese armies could not live off the land, instead they depended on incredibly long supply lines, challenging and vulnerable to being cut or plundered by Xiongnu raiders. Starvation thus became a weapon to strike at the Chinese enemy.

Acting like a guerilla force, the Xiongnu exploited their terrain to the fullest – this would become critical to Yizhixie's evolving strategy against the Han.

Yizhixie in the Field

Soon after securing his *chanyu* title, Yizhixie responded to the recent Han incursions with campaigns of his own. This not only served an immediate military need but also helped shore up his position. In his quest for the throne, it is very likely that he accumulated debts to his supporters and plunder could pay those off. He would also wish to initiate his reign with grand gestures of strength. Just as Modun had done after deposing his father Touman, now Yizhixie needed to prove he was the best man to lead his people to victory.

After massing 30,000 troops, in 125 BC he launched an ambitious three-pronged campaign into the Chinese border provinces of Dai, Dingxiang, and Shang. Details are scanty, but it seems these actions killed and captured a sizable number of Chinese soldiers and civilians. True to their doctrine, the Xiongnu afterwards melted back into their own lands before Han reaction forces could engage them. Perhaps Yizhixie hoped this might snap the Han from their determined course of offensive warfare, but they did not relent. So he campaigned again in 123 BC, and in this the *chanyu* scored an important gain through the Xiongnu talent for integrating defectors.

The *chanyu* and his army cornered a small force commanded by Zhao Xin. A Xiongnu who had formerly defected to the Han and previously served under the general Wei Qing, Zhao's 3,000 troops stood little chance of surviving the clash with his former people. Yizhixie promised Zhao good treatment, and the Han officer, accompanied by 800 of his remaining soldiers, went back over to the Xiongnu. His store of knowledge would later prove tantalizing, and as a sign of his trust and appreciation, Yizhixie made Zhao a king and bestowed a fort upon him.

While the *chanyu* had gained a valuable man in Zhao Xin, the Han also sought defectors. Soon, Yizhixie would lose far more through this.

A Haemorrhage of Land and Men

When in his 174 BC letter the *chanyu* Modun boasted to the Han of defeating the nomadic Yuezhi people, he told also of gaining control of the Tarim Basin (now modern Kazakhstan and Xinjiang Uyghur Autonomous Region, China). This was a section of the Taklamakan Desert which, unlike the rest of that sand sea, supported agriculture and cities through its numerous oases. Several dozen kingdoms grew rich in that region, primarily through trade with points west. Too small to resist the Xiongnu individually and too fractious to band together against the threat, the city-states sank into the Xiongnu sphere of influence.

The Tarim kingdoms, as allies and vassals, buttressed the Xiongnu empire in multiple ways. They provided a steady flow of the fruits of settled society, such as grain and other commodities. The taxes they paid filled the imperial treasury. And for the Xiongnu, always vulnerable to the shocks of losing soldiers, the fighting men of the Tarim kingdoms could be levied as needed. The statelets furnished a buffer, a strategic resource pool the Xiongnu could tap when Han pressures mounted uncomfortably against them. Were they to lose their grip on the region, the Xiongnu would be cut off from vital support, arguably a key element of their ability to wage all-out war with the Han in the costly recent years.

Later, the Tarim Basin emerged as a major theatre in the war, largely through a terrible miscalculation made by Yizhixie. Since he took the throne, Xiongnu performance on the battlefield had at best achieved a stalemate against their adversaries, but on balance – particularly when considering their hindered ability to compensate for their casualties – the Xiongnu were losing. And a Chinese general named Huo Qubing had been the cause of many recent Xiongnu defeats, especially of the Xiongnu 'Hunye king' who was charged with protecting the western domain, including the critical Hexi Corridor. In his battle against the Chinese general, the Hunye king lost between 20,000 and 30,000 men. Furious, in 121 BC Yizhixie demanded he report to him, and either explicitly threatened or clearly intimated his desire that the king answer for his incompetence with his life.

Unfortunately for the *chanyu* and his people, he ought to have better concealed his intentions. Rather than face execution, the Hunye king, along with another tribal sovereign, the Xiutu king, chose to defect to the Chinese.

Not only did they surrender a huge range of territory – the Xiongnu access point to the Tarim Basin and all the wealth they extracted from there – they took with them 40,000 soldiers.

These were stunning blows to Yizhixie. A hole had been punched through the shield of Xiongnu terrain, making incursions deep into his domains more easily launched by his enemies. A major blow to imperial authority, Yizhixie's standing among his subjects certainly suffered, setting a process in train which could lead to more crippling losses of lands. A loose form of monarchy coupled with subjects who could, by dint of their nomadism, simply quit a region wholesale, set the conditions for a potential domino effect of defections, the example set by Yizhixie's Prince Yudan a shining example to disaffected Xiongnu subjects that the Chinese would accommodate them.

The dangers mounted. Losing the Hexi Corridor closed off easy access to the west, leaving only slow, onerous mountain routes. This cut communication between the Xiongnu and potential allies to the northwest, such as the Qiang tribes on the Tibetan Plateau, what could have grown into a mighty alliance against the Han now strangled in its crib. Perhaps most disastrously, Yizhixie's hold on the Tarim Basin now fell under threat. What had been their buffer against the Han, whose resources always dwarfed those of the Xiongnu, now stood in reach of the Chinese.

Now more than ever, reviving the marriage alliance before the Xiongnu lost all credibility as a threat must have dominated the *chanyu*'s thoughts. In a bid to announce his resolve to both the Xiongnu and the Han, at the autumn assembly of 120 BC Yizhixie rallied his soldiers to the warpath. The raiders plunged into the Han frontier regions of Youbeiping and Dingxiang, killing and enslaving approximately 1,000 people. While Xiongnu casualties are unknown, the relatively small scale of Han losses suggests Yizhixie's Xiongnu were dwindling into a spent force; perhaps the *chanyu* would have been wise to wait and gather strength before launching his incursions. For when he dispatched an envoy to the Chinese seeking a return to the old peace, perhaps even with more attractive terms to the Han than previously existed, he was rebuffed. Yizhixie needed some new means to inflict pain on them, that they might see the wisdom of ending the war. Emboldened by their recent successes, perhaps the Han would now overreach, and their tremendous momentum could be turned against them.

Setting a Trap for the Han

With the recent Han territorial gains and their willingness to launch long-distance strikes into Xiongnu territory, fresh eyes and new thinking were required. The acquisition of Zhao Xin, the Xiongnu turned Han officer turned Xiongnu king, granted Yizhixie an advisor holding unique perspective and intelligence on the enemy's capabilities and weaknesses. Zhao Xin advised that the *chanyu* continue to use territory as a weapon, but to sharpen its deadly edges by baiting Han soldiers into venturing farther than they ever had before. If Yizhixie pulled his forces to the northern edge of the Gobi Desert, the Han would be fools to come and fight them there. Zhao promised that the 'Han army has no notion of the difficulties of crossing the immense desert. After crossing, their men and horses will be totally exhausted.'[3]

By shifting to a purely defensive posture, the Xiongnu might lure the Han ever deeper into terrain hostile to life, far from their regional bases and supply chains. Then those soldiers who survived the traversal could be threshed like desiccated stalks of wheat. But would the Han fall for the trap?

Chapter VI

Wei Qing (d. 105 BC): Strategist of the Battlefield and Court

The trap proposed by Zhao Xin drew on his experience of how the Han operated, and perhaps specifically his personal knowledge of one man: the famed general Wei Qing, under whom the Xiongnu defector had fought. Overcoming such a prepared action would take a leader of organization and steadiness, one who had been prophesied to achieve greatness.

A Destiny Foretold

When he was young, Wei Qing met a man – a prisoner in fetters – who claimed to read destinies in faces. In Wei's he glimpsed the glorious future of a marquis. At this the boy laughed. 'I am a slave and getting through the day without punishment is enough for me, let alone becoming a nobleman!'[1]

Unfortunately for the Xiongnu, the soothsayer's prediction came to pass, and the boy slave did one day earn enfeoffment by the emperor for the crippling blows he struck against them. Born in Shanxi ('West of the Mountains') Province, he was the illegitimate son of a government clerk. His low birth meant taking his mother's surname, torment from his legitimate half-brothers, and menial duties, including working as a shepherd.

Nonetheless, his family held connections and his sister secured a position in the harem of Emperor Wu. On her coat-tails Wei's fortunes transformed, gaining him admission into the imperial guard. Yet his presence nearly earned him an early death. Caught up in an intrigue of his half-sister, a princess kidnapped him, intending to kill the young man. But to his rescue charged his friend Gongsun Ao, another army officer. Perhaps as a corrective to the princess's scheming, the emperor lavished Wei with conspicuous gifts and promoted him to high military rank and court position.

Soon Wei saw service. No anecdotes of his performance in his early postings are known, but when the Han launched its first campaign against the Xiongnu in 129 BC, Wei commanded one of the four columns, alongside Li Guang and Wei's friend Gongsun Ao. Wei's column, which included chariots and cavalry, penetrated deep into Xiongnu territory, piercing all the way to the headquarters of Dragon Fort. Wei slew or took prisoner 700 Xiongnu.

It is unknown whether at this point the Xiongnu-turned-Han officer Zhao Xin already served under Wei, but if he did accompany him in this campaign, perhaps he or another Xiongnu provided combat intelligence, analysed enemy actions, or guided the army toward optimal routes for the incursion. In that stark expanse, Wei might also have simply been lucky to contact the enemy. Regardless, Wei's performance was a decidedly different outcome from two of his fellow generals: his friend Gongsun Ao, who failed to make contact with the enemy at all, and Li Guang, who lost men and barely escaped with his life. Both nearly faced capital punishment for this failure.

The distinctions between General Wei and General Li stretched beyond this particular campaign. Where Li Guang was both brash and tongue-tied, an awkward courtier, Li seemed to roam the court as a prime political animal, his deference and protocol towards his superiors in the imperial bureaucracy faultless. It made for a precarious path to walk, to be outstanding yet humble and innocuous, perceived as dangerous to enemies but not to the throne. Yet this balance seemed to come naturally to Wei, whom Sima Qian characterized as self-effacing yet also skilled at currying favour with the emperor. Sima, who surely knew the man personally, did not disguise his opinion, however: 'Yet no one in the empire had a good word to say for him'.[2]

Upon his triumphant return to Chang'an, the prophecy given by the convict face-reader was fulfilled: Wei Qing, the boy who had been born little more than a slave, was enfeoffed as a marquis by the emperor.

Generalship and the Force of Bureaucracy

From the earliest era of recorded Chinese warfare to Wei Qing's day, a general's role simultaneously weakened and grew more professional. Initially leading from the front during the eras of aristocratic warfare, in the Warring States period generals turned to directing battles from a safer vantage than amid the front ranks, their ability with sword or halberd no longer of great matter. In this period demand surged for effective military leaders. A class of roving officers selling both strategic guidance and hands-on command of armies sprang up, their services available to kingly employers. A general's functions became more clarified than in the past; in the field, though they served sovereigns, their authority neared full autonomy, as illustrated in a story about Sun Tzu, author of *The Art of War*.

Peddling his military expertise during the fifth century BC as states fulminated in almost unending conflict, Sun Tzu auditioned for a position as military advisor to a king by demonstrating his methods. Sun Tzu formed

Wei Qing (d. 105 BC): Strategist of the Battlefield and Court

the king's concubines into an army with two units, each with one of the king's favourites serving as their officers. Sun Tzu would be the general, invested with full authority. When he gave orders, the concubine-soldiers giggled and the mock manoeuvres went nowhere. Then, suddenly, the stakes of this demonstration rose considerably. Blaming the 'officers' for dereliction, Sun Tzu summarily ordered their execution. Naturally, the king protested but stood down, acknowledging he had indeed granted a general's sacrosanct authority to Sun Tzu. After the executions took place, the mock army quickly fell into line.

For a general like Wei Qing, such a degree of autonomy truly belonged to another age. In the time of Sun Tzu, the states were smaller, and so were their war aims. Armies pursued territorial expansion far less than securing acknowledgement as being militarily superior by the defeated. A residue of a more individualized, honour-based warfare remained.

In the bureaucratic and paranoid era of the Han, however, generals became even more the instruments of state power, and in turn the state levelled suspicions upon them. Perhaps the upper reaches of the Han government had good reason to worry. Armies of the empire, which at the time of open hostility with the Xiongnu had only just barely overcome multiple open rebellions, provoked anxiety in the court about the loyalties of the men who commanded them. Upon setting out on campaign a general received a tally, often in the shape of a tiger, investing him with command of an army. These tallies were split in two, one half kept by the government so that the pieces could be combined and thus validate the general. It also, perhaps, underscored who the general was beholden to, that it was the court which granted his military authority, symbolically, that without the court the general was merely another Chinese subject.

Therefore, somewhat akin to the power-balancing (or power-neutralizing) method of the early Roman Republic, which alternated commanding generals day to day while on campaign, in most cases two generals held the reins of Han armies. Furthermore, the fact that a general's rank was not permanent but assigned for a specific campaign no doubt helped discourage soldiers from perceiving these men as the bearers of their first loyalty. This in turn supplied a buffer against popular generals from establishing themselves as warlords, a persistent anxiety for an imperial dynasty, especially one in which the sovereign did not dirty his hands with military command.

A more punitive check on a general's ambitions of course existed, as Li Guang at the Battle of Mobei and Wang Hui at the failed Mayi ambush had learned – generals who failed to perform could face the ultimate sanction of death (though luckier ones could buy their lives with hefty fines and reduction in noble rank).

On the battlefield tactical skills meant life or death; in the court, political skills steered one clear of danger. If able to navigate and exploit the bureaucracy, a Han general could thrive as Wei did, or suffer, as did Li Guang. Words and writing marshalled armies, and they lay at the heart of an officer's rise.

An Empire Writing its Way to Conquest

Since the advent of Chinese writing potentially thousands of years before the Han, variant forms abounded. The Qin, striving to unite long-divided and warring peoples, brought a measure of common practices and points of cultural contact throughout their empire by an expansive standardization program. Quelling these variant forms, the Qin established a writing system which could compensate for the fact many Chinese people spoke dialects and, arguably, entirely different languages.

As more people could read and write, and an immense number of Chinese characters joined the language, the bureaucracy could reach ever farther throughout the land. This amplified military strength considerably. Across the empire, troops' call-ups and their allocation to sectors could be closely coordinated. Army officers would have been literate, at least to a degree which enabled them to communicate with their command structure. Combined with an imperial mail system in which galloping messengers could swap their steeds at waystations, writing swelled into a potent Chinese weapon in their fight against a dynamic foe like the Xiongnu.

More Campaigning, More Accolades for Wei

In 128 BC Wei's sister gave birth to the emperor's son, and thereby catapulted from her status as a favoured concubine to the empress of China. Combined with his success in the 129 BC campaign, this must have made Wei the source of much envy by other ambitious commanders; as a marquis and something akin to Emperor Wu's brother-in-law, he could have easily devoted himself to luxury. But instead he continued to venture out into the wilderness in search of the foe. That same year or in 127 BC, he commanded a force of 30,000 cavalry, supported by a sub-commander named Su Jian. Again, Wei located and engaged the enemy, killing and capturing thousands of Xiongnu and seizing an immense amount of livestock. More critically, the Chinese now effectively reoccupied the Ordos Plateau for the first time since it had been captured by Meng Tian of the Qin in 215 BC and subsequently lost to the Xiongnu during the Chu-Han Contention.

Despite Wei Qing's tactical victories, they did not translate to substantial strategic gain. While the loss of men and animals could be harsh setbacks, which the Xiongnu with their small population would struggle to absorb, at the outset of hostilities it was clear how difficult and costly it was to consolidate victory after succeeding in battle. The Han even desisted its expansionism in the northeast and the southwest to concentrate its might on the Xiongnu. Yet they had not significantly degraded the enemy's capacity for war, as Yizhixie's three-pronged operation in 125 BC demonstrated. Emperor Wu's appetite, though, had not been satiated, and while the civil servants in his government increasingly opposed the expensive and arduous war, his cult of personality and his corps of loyal eunuchs meant that, more than his predecessors, he could rule by fiat. His faith was strong in General Wei, and he charged him to respond to those 125 BC incursions.

Placed in command of 30,000 troops, in 124 BC Wei set out. Though the enemy hunkered far to the north, surely in a region they considered safe territory, by some means, whether superior scouting, reliable intelligence, or luck, Wei tracked down the Sage King of the Right and his army.

Perhaps the best way to battle an enemy as elusive as the Xiongnu, as planners of the would-be ambush at Mayi observed, was to allow them to fall into bad habits – and then play their own game of using surprise to devastating effect. Wei Qing certainly capitalized on this by stealing a march on his foe. Discovering the encampment of the Xiongnu force, he and his men approached under the cover of darkness. They surrounded it and struck, catching the unsuspecting Sage King drunk.

Amid the confusion of night fighting, the Xiongnu commander managed to round up his concubines and best men, mount his horse and burst through the Han lines. Despite pursuit by Han cavalry, the fugitive king made good his escape to the north. A near miss for Wei, yet still he captured numerous members of the commander's staff, 15,000 others and a substantial portion of their herds. Surely this would have been a devastating blow to the Xiongnu, leading to much starvation. Wei seemed unable to fail.

Rising High ... Carefully

Delighted by this latest victory, the emperor dispatched an envoy to meet Wei in the field and present seals of office making him a supreme commander, his authority now extending over all other Han generals. Moreover, the former slave boy's good fortune spread to his family, for the emperor expanded the general's holdings and sought also to enfeoff his three sons. Wei, however, declined this honour.

> Unworthy as I am, I have been granted the privilege of riding into battle. Through the divine wisdom of Your Majesty, the army has won a great

victory, but the merit is due wholly to the fighting ability of my officers. Your Majesty has graciously increased my own fief, but my sons are still in swaddling clothes and have performed no service. Though Your Majesty kindly wishes to set aside lands and enfeoff them as well, I fear it would do little to encourage the men who have fought under me.³

Whether out of genuine modesty or an acute sense of self-preserving propriety, Wei perhaps responded wisely. By declining, he potentially signalled a lack of desire to found a powerful political dynasty of his own; he thus avoided some of the poisonous politics of the court. Already he had earned imperial trust and favour, and the emperor's esteem – awards of far greater worth than the income from an enlarged fief. Wei stood so much in the emperor's graces, Emperor Wu would receive him when unadorned in his imperial regalia, and even when he was at his toilet.

Before long Wei's political instincts would be tested again. In response to a Xiongnu raid on the commandery of Dai in the fall of 124 BC, Wei launched a counterattack. He commanded other generals in the operation, including Li Guang who took up the rear, and on the right wing, Su Jian, Wei's sub-commander on previous campaigns. After killing or capturing several thousand enemies, they returned, only to march out a month later with even greater success, this time slaying 10,000. Yet Su Jian's unit hit catastrophe, his entire force slaughtered or captured. He alone stumbled back to headquarters. Of course, Su now faced another lethal danger: Han law.

As general-in-chief, the adjudication fell to Wei. One officer advised he execute Su to demonstrate the authority of his new high office; another warned against this rash act, observing that it would only encourage other officers to surrender to the enemy, if the prize for holding fast against overwhelming odds was to be slain by their own people. Wei opted for a politically balanced tack, neither meting out punishment nor absolving Su Jian, instead deciding the emperor must determine General Su's fate. 'While I have the authority to behead an officer, I do not wish to be seen as exercising that authority in arbitrary fashion', Wei explained – a canny move from a seasoned political player.⁴

More worrying for Wei Qing and the Han military, this was the battle in which Chanyu Yizhixie lured the Xiongnu defector Zhao Xin back to his people. With a store of knowledge on Han tactics and strategic plans, Zhao Xin, as advisor to Yizhixie, developed the gambit of retreating ever farther north. Should the Chinese be foolhardy enough to seek them, any stragglers who survived the crossing would surely be in a wretched and confused state, easily picked off. Unless Wei could find a way to turn the trap on them.

The Battle of Mobei (the Northern Desert)

Zhao Xin knew firsthand the Han's military weaknesses, chief among them the desperate dearth of horses. In operating far from their bases of support, their supply lines were weak, their lack of horses reduced mobility to find the Xiongnu and then to pursue them in the aftermath to consolidate their wins. Based on this, the strategy he proposed to Chanyu Yizhixie was essentially akin to the Romans' 'Fabian strategy' in their war with the Carthaginians – avoiding contact with the Han by withdrawing into the northern domain of the Gobi Desert, allowing the Chinese forces to exhaust and winnow themselves against the harsh environment.

What Wei Qing and the campaign planners conjured to overcome this was not some novel strategy or tactic but making their resources work better for them – and it underscored the strategic advantage China always possessed over their under-resourced enemy. Though perennially short on horses, nevertheless they could put out a call across the empire to gather them. They trotted in from all parts of China, horses from government stables and privately owned animals all pressed into service. To extend their effective range, these horses were gorged and fattened prior to entering the field.

Wei's command of cavalry would have been crucial, even if many Chinese riders lacked the almost inborn proficiency of Xiongnu raised on steppes and plains. The chariots in his command, on the other hand, must have seemed a relic when facing a foe highly mobile over broken ground, but they and the lumbering cargo wagons would help turn the coming battle.

With 100,000 cavalry, in 119 BC Wei set out. Two key generals served under him: Li Guang and Huo Qubing, a masterful mounted archer and Wei's own nephew. In this pair of leaders can be seen the two fickle faces of chance or destiny, for one was to end his run of misfortune in suicide while the other continued his uncontested ascent to greatness. Huo would operate in the eastern theatre of the campaign, Wei the west. Wei assigned Li Guang to protect the right flank, which provoked the lower-ranked general to protest he had been promised the vanguard (as we know, Wei acted under a direct order of Emperor Wu, who declared Li must assume no position of strategic importance).

Wei advanced 1,000 *li* – about 500 kilometres (310 miles) – through the desert fastnesses. The crossing must have been utterly brutal, the sun blazing, the nights freezing, the soldiers aching for the fastidiously rationed water. And then the beleaguered army walked into an ambush.

A basic military posture would have anticipated some sort of attack, yet it appears the Xiongnu caught the Han army by surprise. After the trials the men had endured reaching this place, they must have been at risk of buckling. Only decisive leadership might carry the day. The general quickly ordered his chariots and wagons to form up in a defensive ring (the same tactic used by Li Guang in an earlier battle). This established a basic static defence against the Xiongnu, yet Wei must have known such a passive action alone would only slow the slaughter of his men to Xiongnu arrows, so he dispatched 5,000 riders to engage the enemy. Shielded behind their vehicles, Han crossbowmen and archers released blistering volleys on the charging Xiongnu. Viciously the two sides fought until dusk fell. Surely Wei Qing prayed for reinforcements to ride in and lift the siege. Where was that dawdling Li Guang and his unit? Instead, help blew in from another quarter.

As the sun set, strong winds kicked up a dust storm. The swirling grit blinded Han and Xiongnu alike. While it would seem these conditions would equally affect both sides, here the discipline of a well-drilled Chinese force, guided by superior command and control, turned the tide. Somehow Wei managed to coordinate flanking attacks upon Yizhixie and his army. What ought to have been a great Xiongnu victory turned instead into an embarrassment for the *chanyu*, who, using a team of donkeys, had to make a narrow breakout with his men.

In the aftermath Wei captured 10,000 enemy and also struck a blow against Zhao Xin, who had once been his officer but had turned back to the Xiongnu. Finding Zhao's fort, he demolished it and burned its ample grain stores, surely denying life to many down the line. Combined with Wei's recapture of the Ordos Plateau and the 121 BC defection of the Hunye king, finally the Han achieved profound strategic gains.

A Mausoleum and a Feud

Well after the fighting had finished, General Li Guang stumbled in, completing the rendezvous too late to offer any help in the seminal Battle of Mobei. Never again would he arrive late to a junction, for he chose to take his own life rather than face the judgement of the court. His death sowed bitterness between the Wei and Li clans. Li Guang's son, Li Gan, blamed Wei for his father's death, and later he even assaulted the old general. Wei Qing dismissed the matter, but his nephew Huo Qubing was not so quick to forgive.

When General Wei Qing died in 106 BC (the cause is unrecorded), the great conqueror and favourite of the court merited a last expression of imperial favour: a mausoleum whose construction was personally ordered by Emperor Wu. It took the shape of a mountain within the Xiongnu's range, from the territory of an enemy which had provided Wei Qing the opportunity to rise from a slave boy to a lauded general celebrated by the Son of Heaven.

Chapter VII

Huo Qubing (140–117 BC): Horseman with the Strength of the Steppe

After the Battle of Mobei, the rancour following Li Guang's humiliation and suicide continued to build in his son Li Gan. He directed his ire firmly at Wei Qing, who had potentially deliberately set up his father to fail to make the junction with the main army in the campaign. The grievances spread – Li Gan's attack on Wei Qing did not sit easily with Huo Qubing, Wei Qing's young, hotblooded nephew and, as he so often did in the field, Huo meant to take decisive, lethal action.

In 117 BC, two years after Li Guang's death, Emperor Wu invited both Li Gan and Huo Qubing to join his retinue on a hunting trip. While out stalking prey, Huo took aim not at a fleeing quarry – but at Li Gan. Huo shot him dead.

It was brazen murder of an imperial officer conducted in his majesty's presence. This should have destined the rash young man for execution. Yet special concessions could be made for the masterful cavalry commander. At this stage in Huo's brief career, he had already equalled the victories of his uncle Wei Qing. Huo was too effective and valuable – and adored by his emperor – to let mere murder tamper with his career, and the Son of Heaven simply declared Li Gan had sadly been gored by a stag. An accident.

How did Huo Qubing earn such imperial regard?

Origin and Early Campaigns

Huo Qubing was Wei Qing's nephew through the latter's elder sister. Like Wei Qing, he was raised in Shanxi, and also like him, Huo was both of illegitimate yet highly placed birth, his mother marrying one of Emperor Wu's ministers and his aunt becoming an imperial consort and later the empress. This gave Huo sterling opportunities to be noticed in the court and, coupled with outstanding prowess as a warrior, positioned him for a meteoric rise.

As a Shanxi man, like his uncle, Huo would have honed his horsemanship and archery from a tender age, gaining the skills to make him a worthier adversary to the Xiongnu than soldiers from other regions of the empire. He also accompanied his uncle on his campaigns, giving him the opportunity to learn and refine his skills as a combat commander.

At the age of eighteen he became an attendant in the imperial palace. Somehow, he deeply impressed the emperor. At Emperor Wu's direction, in 123 BC Wei Qing dubbed him 'Swift Commander' and assigned him a unit of 800 young horsemen. Almost immediately, Huo distinguished himself.

In 123 BC he ventured out with his unit attached to a larger army. Straying from the ponderous main force, Huo led his gallants several hundred kilometres ahead on a long-range mission, either a search-and-destroy patrol or a reconnaissance in force. With his small, nimble unit, its footprint and need for support light, he closely matched the Xiongnu way of war. As illustrated by Li Guang's debacles – when he was in command of thousands of men, he never rivalled his success as he had when commanding 100 – these compact units which could meet the Xiongnu on their own terms sometimes punched far above their weight.

Huo's success in his first campaign was immortalized in an imperial edict:

Swift Commander Huo Qubing beheaded or captured 2,280 Xiongnu, among them their chief minister and an official of the royal household, a marquis, and a paternal uncle of the *chanyu*. Within the army no man has earned more distinction. He shall be awarded a feof of 1,600 households and be granted the title of 'Champion of the Army'.[1]

An 18-year-old in his first command could hardly ask for a finer assessment by his emperor. Like his uncle, Huo seemed to enjoy a wonderful fusion of talent and luck.

Huo Qubing and Li Guang – Cut from the Same Cloth?

Huo's early enfeoffment contrasts dramatically with the trajectory of Li Guang, who to the soothsayer had bemoaned how his junior officers earned plaudits while he went unrewarded. Yet striking parallels exist between Huo and Li Guang, the father of the man he murdered. Both were audacious horsemen from the frontier, skilled with the bow, more comfortable fighting and leading from the front than perhaps the more controlled and disciplined Wei Qing. 'General Huo Qubing was a laconic man', observed Sima Qian, 'valiant and bold'.[2]

Further, Huo appeared to fight by instinct, not through schooled military science. When the emperor tried to teach him about the strategies of Sun Tzu and other luminaries of military thought from the Warring States era, Huo scoffed. 'What good is this so-called strategy over action? There is nothing to learn from those ancients.'³ (In the young man's defence, it probably was farcical for the pampered emperor to attempt schooling a war hero in the realities of combat.)

Despite his lack of polish, Emperor Wu cherished Huo, and one way he demonstrated this favour emphasized the great gulf yawning between Huo and Li Guang. Though resupply was one of the most pressing logistical worries of all Han campaigns, the emperor ensured that Huo received the finest provisions, sending his personal steward to deliver twenty or more wagons crammed with delicacies for the young cavalryman's pleasure. In a famous incident celebrated through the centuries, when a fine wine had been sent to him, Huo poured it into a spring, so that all his men might share alike of the emperor's gift. This place became known as Jiuquan ('Wine Spring'), a vital staging ground for the war in the northwestern theatre.

Yet one point of contrast shows a very different leader from Li Guang. When those wagons filled with provisions returned to the capital, Huo had hardly put a dent in the food, while his own men staggered home half-starved – a far cry from Li Guang's sharing the undoubtedly rotting rations of his men. When at camp, Huo sometimes ordered his exhausted soldiers to play *cuju* (a sort of ancient Chinese football) for his entertainment. Where the older general was beloved throughout the ranks, Sima Qian took a withering position against Huo's arrogant and selfish manner, claiming that after his rise to stratospheric rank he cared little for the welfare of his troops.

Inflicting Haemorrhage on the Foe

In 121 BC Huo's star had risen to the point that he now, at around the age of 19 or 20, took command of 10,000 horsemen. Considering the advanced ages of Li Guang and Wei Qing, clearly Huo enjoyed a signal honour to be so charged. But could he replicate the successes he'd enjoyed with 800 men when leading a force a dozen times larger? He set out from Beidi along with the general Gongsun Ao, with the intention to make a later rendezvous. The units could not make contact, however, so Huo forged far ahead. Unreinforced, he nonetheless took the fight to the enemy. The emperor later announced:

> The general of swift cavalry Huo Qubing has led his fighting men across Mount Wuli and struck at the tribes of Supu; he has crossed the Hunu River and marched through the lands of five barbarian rulers with his baggage trains and hosts of followers, sparing only those who submitted in fear before him. Hoping to capture the son of the *Shanyu*, he fought a

running battle for six days, riding 1,000 *li* or more beyond Mount Yanzhi, meeting the enemy in close combat, killing the ruler of Lan, slaying the barbarian King Lu, wiping out the entire enemy force and capturing the son of the Hunye king and his ministers and chief commandants. He has killed and captured over 8,000 of the enemy and seized the golden man which the Xiutu king uses in worshipping Heaven.[4]

This campaign shook the Xiongnu at their roots, setting the disastrous events in train which culminated in Chanyu Yizhixie's rash decision to order the execution of the Hunye king in response to Huo's repeated victories against him. This in turn touched off defections the empire would struggle to recover from. After the Hunye king declared his intention to surrender to the Han, the emperor, fearing this was only a devious prelude to an attack, dispatched Huo to verify the king's conviction. Upon seeing the Han army, the king and his core followers submitted. But some in his army did not wish to become vassals of the Han and either sought to escape or engage their sworn enemy. General Huo launched an attack, his army killing or capturing more than 8,000 of the enemy and 32 tribal kings. The remaining 100,000 Xiongnu submitted.

The Hunye king had controlled the western domain of the Xiongnu empire, certainly their most valuable territory due to its communication via the Hexi Corridor to the wealthy Tarim Basin. With these vital areas under Han control, the Chinese sealed off their flank and created the opening for further western expansion. It gifted the emperor with the chance to reduce spending along the border, for with the immediate Xiongnu threat somewhat de-fanged, garrison forces could be lightened by half, reducing the costs for an eye-wateringly expensive war.

The Chinese empire pulled off a profound coup with this and Huo Qubing bore significant responsibility. In reward for Huo's triumph, his fiefs were expanded, making him an exceedingly wealthy man. What accounted for his extraordinary accomplishments? One factor contributed more than any other.

Drawing Influence from the Steppe

Between his background as a man from the edge of the steppe and his aptitude as a mounted archer, Huo adapted Xiongnu techniques and tactical thinking. He understood ancient 'manoeuvre warfare' inherently, it seems, in ways those beholden to the precepts of Sun Tzu and others, founded on an infantry-centric model of war, could not. Into his brand of warfare he incorporated the military culture of the steppe, making it acceptable and possible for the Chinese. The steppe was like a potent, supercharging force, one which Chinese warriors drew from to gain combat prowess – but too much ran the risk of 'going barbarian' and breeding questionable loyalties.

The paired weapon system of horse and composite bow found their way into Chinese use through the steppe. In 307 BC King Wuling of Zhao, a state far to the north, bordering the Ordos region, incorporated military elements from the various nomadic groups he struggled against (perhaps the Xiongnu among them). He commanded his horsemen to wear trousers as the barbarians did, far better suited to sitting astride horses than their traditional robes, and he insisted his men train in barbarian tactics and archery. A fair number of those who had horses might have fought not as cavalry but as mounted infantry, riding to battles and then dismounting to fight on foot, though still the advantages in speed and range would have been immense.

As an obvious favourite of the emperor, Huo Qubing enjoyed his pick of the finest riders available. While the older generals jockeyed for men and horses, Huo received all he requested. Likely a sizeable portion of Huo's force was made up of Xiongnu as well; at least one of his sub-commanders was. With the Xiongnu weak on imperial ideology, a charismatic figure like Huo, superb as a mounted archer, could surely sway some of them to his banner, particularly if he could deliver what the *chanyu* would have promised these men – plunder and glory. These Xiongnu warriors of course thrived in this combat context and also held 'institutional knowledge' of the foe, perhaps came into fresher critical intelligence, and could help Huo analyse developments in real time.

Like the Xiongnu, who could execute lightning raids and disappear before a Han reaction force even mustered, Huo understood the primacy of speed. Freed from leading cumbersome chariots, his smaller, capable forces could likely live off the land, or at least subsist on limited provisions. Yet all this depended on access to one limited, vital resource.

Horses in China

While China could conscript huge numbers of men to fill army ranks, mass-produce quality arms and armour, and tempt Xiongnu defectors with hefty payouts, it struggled to raise horses of the quality and quantity necessary to mount expeditionary campaigns year after year. In a plain demonstration that these animals were more valuable than men, conscripts could dodge their service if they substituted horses for themselves.

Beyond lacking speed to force contact with the enemy, infantrymen cannot effectively withdraw from combat with a mounted foe. On the other hand, Xiongnu, unless fully encircled, could often disengage from a battle turning against them. As the Han had learned already in several engagements, the lack of a well-equipped cavalry meant that successful battles failed to build into true victory, as Xiongnu leaders and their men frequently slipped away to fight another day.

The clear admiration Emperor Wu showed for Huo Qubing meant his success, as his access to resources, especially quality horses, was both instrumental to the young general's success and an enviable position for a Han soldier. China lacked robust horse stocks and pasturage was thin; among other motives for seizing Xiongnu territory, the means to breed healthy, abundant herds must have ranked high among the Han. Indeed, soon the hunt for horses would spur Chinese exploration and conquest.

Back to Campaigning

Following Huo's brilliant turn in 121 BC leading to the fragmentation of the Xiongnu through the Hunye king's defection, in the summer of that same year Huo again launched a strike deep into enemy territory. In typical Han fashion, the plan called for two units to rendezvous in the field, but they did not manage this. Nonetheless, Huo carried on alone to the Qilian Mountains, a range which formed the southern edge of the Hexi Corridor. Emperor Wu's edict enumerates his success: after capturing the king of the Qiutu (one of the affiliated Xiongnu tribes), 2,500 of the king's men surrendered. Then:

> Huo Qubing beheaded or captured more than 30,000 of the enemy, and seized 5 kings and 5 queen mothers, 59 princes and other royals, 63 high officials, generals, and other high-ranking officers. He lost only 3 tenths of his own soldiers in these actions.[5]

As a participant in the Northern Desert campaign, assigned to the eastern battlespace, Huo set another jewel in his crown. He rode out of the strongholds of Dai and Youbeiping along the border with a whopping 50,000, which included many captured and defected Xiongnu, including 2 kings with their armed retinues. Unlike most of his fellow commanders, Huo was permitted to operate without any additional generals in his force, no checks on him, his command absolute. Instead, he placed men like Li Gan, Li Guang's son, in positions of authority.

Emperor Wu issued an edict to capture General Huo's exploits for posterity:

> The general of swift cavalry has led forth the troops and personally commanded a force of barbarians captured in previous campaigns, carrying with him only light provisions and crossing the great desert.

Huo Qubing (140–117 BC): Horseman with the Strength of the Steppe

Fording the Huozhangqu, he executed the enemy leader Bijuqi and then turned to strike at the enemy general of the left, cutting down his pennants and seizing his war drums.[6]

Bursting onward, he captured 3 Xiongnu kings, 83 generals and other officials, on top of a suspiciously exact number of other prisoners, 70,443.

Huo's star could hardly rise higher. Together with Wei Qing he earned a rank devised by the emperor of 'grand marshal'. The nephew was outshining his famous uncle and Huo further usurped his standing by welcoming Wei's officers – some of whom had been his old comrades – to his own command. Serving under Huo became an attractive billet, with the promise of rewards granted by the emperor, who attentively followed the young general's exploits. Even Li Gan prospered under Huo, decorated in this campaign for capturing standards and drums of the enemy. While his father's failure in the campaign drove him to suicide, Li Gan earned a marquisate, that accolade his father had long sought for himself. However, while Li Gan served with distinction under Huo and was honoured by Emperor Wu, this would not save him from the 'hunting accident' and the emperor's coverup of the murder.

Conquests Beyond the Horizon

After Huo's last victory, he led a sacred rite almost always reserved for emperors to perform, the *feng* and *shan* sacrifices. For the *feng*, Huo scaled a mountain in the region and at its peak offered a sacrifice in tribute to Heaven. At the foot of another mountain, he made the *shan* offering, here paying homage to Earth. In conducting the rites, he in essence sanctified these heretofore-contested lands as Chinese soil. And by standing in for the emperor, he announced his towering stature within the court. It was a monumental capstone to an astounding career.

In a brief, concentrated burst of activity, Huo had achieved incredible success and played a singular role in sapping the Xiongnu. Though celebrated and rich, very likely Huo would not have sat on his laurels but continued his long-distance strikes against the enemy, for when the emperor offered to build his firebrand general a mansion, Huo retorted, 'While the Xiongnu have still not been wiped out there is no time to think about houses!'[7] It hardly mattered for in 117 BC Emperor Wu did not decree the construction of a home for him, rather of a tomb.

At the age of 23 Huo Qubing died. The manner of his demise is unknown, though it would seem not in combat as that would most likely have been memorialized in the annals. A grieving Emperor Wu ordered a massive memorial effort. Along an approximately 40-kilometre road, captured and defected Xiongnu lined up holding iron weapons as his body processed past. Huo was interred in a sepulchre shaped like the Qilian Mountains, where he had won a great victory along the Hexi Corridor. His actions against the enemy were further commemorated in a statue at his tomb, with a horse trampling a cowering Xiongnu warrior.

Huo's legacy was immense, and the lessons for the Han deep. His actions demonstrated how a daring, aggressive method of making war could bring powerful results. His body blows against the Xiongnu engendering the defection of the Hunye king from the Xiongnu to the Han, knocked the steppe empire back on its heels and steered the war towards the west, opening a new front in the conflict. His many successes rested on access to quality horses and to using turned Xiongnu as allies. The pursuit of both fuelled continuing Han war aims and the far-flung exploits of two Chinese generals and a resourceful peace bride who immortalized their names by exploring, conquering, and sealing alliances with new nations in the lands of the westering sun.

Part Three

Pathfinders to the West

Items like this belt buckle are among the few surviving relics fashioned by Xiongnu hands.

A Xiongnu crown from the Warring States period. The Xiongnu were renowned for their metalworking skill.

Emperor Gaozu (Liu Bang), the founder of the Han dynasty with a 'face like a dragon'.

Emperor Wu of Han. His decision to end the decades-long policy of appeasement by marriage alliance changed the face of Chinese-Xiongnu relations and ushered in centuries of war.

A Han military command tally. At the start of campaigning a general received this symbol of his authority, retaining it for the duration of field operations.

Possible Xiongnu sword.

Replica of Han lamellar armour. Advanced metallurgy and mass-production meant many Chinese soldiers took the field well-equipped.

Detail of Han crossbowmen on architectural model of watchtower. While the crossbow revolutionized warfare for the Chinese, the Xiongnu did not adopt this weapon.

A Han chariot. Precisely how it was used on the battlefield remains a mystery, though it is evident that the flexibility, speed, and manoeuvrability of the mounted Xiongnu brought the chariot's military role largely to an end.

Han horse sculpture. China's need to bolster its weak stock of horses fuelled trade, diplomacy, and warfare with its Central Asian neighbours.

Architectural model of a Han watchtower. Soldiers stood long, lonely watches scouring for Xiongnu while on garrison duty.

The Han-dynasty Great Wall. It was constructed primarily of rammed earth rather than the brick of more recent eras. (慕尼黑啤酒 *via Wikimedia Commons/CC BY-SA 3.0*)

Both praised and persecuted in his day, and revered in the millennia since, the historian Sima Qian gave firsthand accounts of significant figures and events of the Han-Xiongnu War.

Scholar-officials. A vast bureaucracy grew entrenched in the Han dynasty, with a variety of effects on the prosecution of war by the empire.

Statue of a horse stomping a Xiongnu at the tomb of General Huo Qubing.

Fresco of Zhang Qian and Emperor Wu. Zhang's western expeditions helped open both Chinese trade routes and new theatres of the Han-Xiongnu War.

Fresco showing golden statues, booty from a campaign against the Xiongnu.

This textile from the Tarim Basin shows a soldier of likely Hellenic descent. Greek cultural influence persisted for centuries at the fringes of Chinese civilization.

Textile from Xiongnu tomb depicting Yuezhi warriors battling Sogdians.

The Inscription of Yanran commemorating final defeat of the Xiongnu. Ban Gu composed the text a few years before suffering imprisonment due to his association with disgraced Han general Dou Xian. (*Badamsambu via Wikimedia Commons/CC BY-SA 4.0*)

Chapter VIII

Zhang Qian (died c. 114 BC): Pioneer of the Silk Road

A famous *chengyu*, or saying, reflects the Chinese desire to turn enemies against one another rather than become directly involved with combat: 'Use barbarians to fight barbarians'. At first a mere aspiration, with Han successes on the battlefield and dissension within Xiongnu ranks, it grew into a time-honoured Chinese strategy and policy.

A metaphorical conception of geography by the ancient Chinese hints at their understanding of their place in the world and the position of foreigners. They viewed themselves as living with the 'Four Seas', these being the South and East China Seas, to the west, Qinghai Lake on the Tibetan plateau and, as the northern extremity, Lake Baikal in Siberia. These were the border points of Chinese consciousness and beyond them lay the *terra incognita* of the 'Eight Wastes', benighted lands inhabited by the rawest of barbarians, far from the flame of Chinese civilization. At the same time *tianxia*, 'all under Heaven', a core governing principle for the empire, contended that foreign peoples could be incorporated into the Chinese cultural sphere so long as they paid tribute to the throne – acknowledging that the emperor, the Son of Heaven, was the supreme lawgiver and true source of the Chinese right to rule. Should they wish it, foreign lands could also opt for direct Chinese rule and accept colonization. In some ways *tianxia* thus acted as a form of manifest destiny. These conceptions of the wider world also laid an intellectual foundation for seeking allies in distant lands.

To the Han, who feared internal threats far more than the Xiongnu, arming and training their own people was a regrettable necessity. Men versed in the profession of arms held both the fighting and the organizational skills to challenge the throne. Engaging the enemy with combat assets which were far from one's own vulnerable heartland, therefore, offered a handsome alternative. And not coincidentally, these tribal peoples had ample supplies of horses.

Huo Qubing's successes proclaimed the importance of horses and the value of using indigenous forces on campaign. Of course, these were not revelations to the Han, and well before Huo first went to battle Chinese envoys travelled north and west in search of horses and allies. In the years before Mayi, angling to overturn the embarrassing marriage alliances, Emperor Wu sought to strengthen his hand before opening large-scale hostilities against the Xiongnu. And the Han knew the importance of allies for their coming war. The likeliest group to cultivate was one with enduring enmity toward the Xiongnu, and who had in the previous century made vassals of them: the Yuezhi.

Courting an Unknown People

It was the Yuezhi who had held the young Modun as a hostage and lorded power over the Xiongnu after they had been displaced from the Ordos by Qin aggression. The Yuezhi fought as the Xiongnu did, primarily as mounted archers. With Han horse shortages and a lack of a military culture around mounted warfare, the prospect of recruiting a horde of such fighters must have been irresistible. Soon after first sitting on the Dragon Throne in 141 BC, Emperor Wu questioned captive and turncoat Xiongnu; from them he learned that in 166 BC their *chanyu*, Laoshang (the son and heir of Modun), had captured the Yuezhi chief and made a drinking vessel of his skull. Perhaps such a bloody history spelled opportunity for the Han? Someone must cross Xiongnu territory, brave natural dangers, Xiongnu and bandits, find the Yuezhi nation and persuade them to seek vengeance on the Xiongnu.

For this delicate and dangerous mission, the emperor selected a man named Zhang Qian. By some means Zhang had become an attendant of the Chang'an court, and possibly climbed the ranks to become captain of the palace guard. When the call for a mission to the Yuezhi came, he answered. No doubt it held great promise for fame, wealth and other rewards.

What qualified Zhang for this assignment? Sima Qian, who surely knew him personally, wrote that Zhang was 'of great strength, generous, and trustworthy – and the barbarian peoples adored him'.[1] He shared a geographic heritage with other prominent Chinese generals, hailing from Shaanxi, a frontier region, from a town named Cheng Gu. Shaanxi was both the seat of government and the edge of the steppe, so it might have provided the unique background Zhang required for his task. Perhaps he had exposure to nomadic peoples, gaining some familiarity with their ways. Perhaps he had gathered proficiency with a language used by the Xiongnu or other people of that region. Such skills, most likely a combination of horsemanship, survival abilities in harsh terrain, proficiency with arms, and language abilities all would come into play – but perhaps most of all, a diplomatic tongue.

Notably, as the expedition was being prepared – around 140 BC – the Han had not initiated full-blown hostilities against the Xiongnu and the marriage alliance still nominally maintained the peace between the societies (the failed ambush at Mayi would occur in 133 BC, at last shattering the strained peace). It was a secret diplomatic mission, for were the Xiongnu to discover the embassy, it might tip too much of the Han's hand, and its brewing intentions. And so the posture of the expedition, while surely it went armed to defend itself, was not for war, and most likely gifts and money to impress tribesmen outnumbered weaponry.

Zhang outfitted his embassy with more than one hundred men. Surely some soldiers were included, and also translators, traders, perhaps some proto-naturalists seeking unusual specimens. Certainly, the most valuable among his retinue was Ganfu, a surrendered or captive Xiongnu and Zhang's slave, who would serve as the expedition's guide. If any reminder were needed of the mission's object, this alone told resoundingly how valuable Xiongnu turned to the Han could be when operating in this theatre, whether for diplomacy or war.

With Ganfu at the head, in 139 or 138 BC Zhang and his caravan set out from Gansu, travelling along the northern edge of the Hexi Corridor. Upon reaching Yumen, the Jade Gate (now in China's Gansu Province), the main egress to the passage west, they slipped outside the bounds of Chinese protection.

An excellent archer, Ganfu supplemented their provisions by hunting game, and likely the small size of the expedition, compared to a massive army column, meant they were better able to live off the land when traversing the long stretches between settlements. No doubt Ganfu guided them through lands with Xiongnu least disposed towards preying on them. Nevertheless, almost immediately, Zhang's mission took an unlucky turn – he fell into the hands of the Xiongnu.

A Xiongnu Family Man

The strange nature of this caravan must have been difficult to conceal from those who discovered them, and Zhang and his retinue were brought to Chanyu Junchen. Whether Zhang or other travellers revealed the object of their mission or not, Junchen clearly understood its import: 'To the north of these lands live the Yuezhi,' he said. 'And the Han hope to send an envoy to them? Were I to send envoys to the nations south of China, would they be granted safe passage through Chinese land?'[2] The *chanyu* made a valid point, and accordingly Zhang and the others became his prisoners.

Thus began a long stretch in Zhang's life imbued with mystery. In an era of regular correspondence between sovereigns there is seemingly no record of the *chanyu* seeking to ransom Zhang or the like from the imperial court. Frustratingly, almost nothing is known of the conditions in which he was kept, though it is difficult to imagine a nomadic society, likely going through periods of living hand to mouth, wasting resources on keeping a prisoner in fetters for years, so perhaps he became a contributing member of the community in some fashion. At the very least, he contributed to their numbers: Zhang married a Xiongnu woman who bore him a son.

As the Han feared and sought to contain from the first, a rich tradition persisted of Han subjects going over to the other side, so there was sufficient fluidity in the Xiongnu culture to find a place for Zhang. It must be remembered this was a multi-ethnic, multilingual and largely tolerant society, so perhaps Zhang's background was eventually overlooked and he slowly integrated. Indeed, Zhang might have 'defected' after a fashion. Obviously, his position was a different one from say, Zhonghang Yue, the embittered eunuch who advised Chanyu Laoshang in 166 BC to mount a massive incursion into China. Still though, settled there with a family, Zhang could have faced temptations to truly make a life among his keepers. That he was able to find a place in their community, albeit unwillingly at least at first, reinforces how capably the Xiongnu accepted Chinese in their community.

While Zhang spent nine or ten years among the Xiongnu, Sima Qian in two paragraphs relates this entire period, though this chapter of Zhang's life must have been bursting with incident. It would have been a tantalizing record of Xiongnu daily life which Zhang could have offered, an eyewitness account to Xiongnu mores which no one else was qualified to provide.

The discovery of the Han's diplomatic secret mission likely put the Xiongnu on heightened alert after this naked attempt to forge an alliance with their hated enemy. It is interesting to speculate whether the discovery of Zhang's mission played into the Xiongnu detecting the attempted Han trap at Mayi in 133 BC. Obviously Zhang had no knowledge of it, though it might have put the Xiongnu on notice that the Chinese were striving for a response to them more ambitious than simply manning their border garrisons. And over the course of Zhang's captivity, huge forces were at play, shifting the dynamic between the two empires.

Circa 130 BC, the decade-long sojourn came to an end without Sima Qian revealing anything more regarding Zhang's circumstances among the Xiongnu. He recorded that throughout 'this time [Zhang] had kept possession of the Emperor's token of authority, and, when in the course of time he was allowed greater liberty, he, watching his opportunity, succeeded in making his escape'.[3] Further details are missing, though it is known that Ganfu, his Xiongnu slave, accompanied him. Sources offer contradictory accounts regarding whether Zhang's wife and son also abandoned their community. Such knowledge might have shed light on his captivity's complexion.

Back on the Path

One wonders upon his escape, what possible moves Zhang considered. His mission was now ten years delayed. Perhaps he had a sense of the wider conflict which now boiled between the Han and Xiongnu. If he returned to China emptyhanded, he might elude punishment but surely his career would be forever stalled. So, still possessing his imperial credentials, he opted to resume his journey west. Twenty or thirty days of travel brought Zhang, Ganfu, and whoever else remained of the original expedition to the Ferghana Valley (the eastern region of modern Uzbekistan). The civilization he found there must have startled him.

Its people looked at him with their deep-set eyes. They drank grape wine, and their culture showed other vestiges of some distant western territory. Zhang had come to the lands of what the Chinese called the Dayuan ('Great Greek') kingdom. Once a Hellenistic society, it had been colonized by soldiers of Alexander the Great's conquests through the region. But at some point had come the Saka people, Iranian nomads who subjugated Dayuan. (Sima Qian notes that their 'arms consist of bows and halberds, and they shoot arrows while on horseback'[4] – practices more consistent with nomadic tactics.) The nomads became overlords of the farmers and traders. Over time Dayuan's Hellenistic traits began to fade, though still an envoy of a Chinese Confucian court had contacted a civilization derived from Hellenistic culture – a wondrous meeting brought about by the overarching conflict between Chinese and Xiongnu.

Theirs was a highly urbanized society: the people of Dayuan 'have walled cities and houses; the large and small cities belonging to them fully seventy in number, contain an aggregate population of several hundreds of thousands', wrote Sima Qian.[5] The scale of their civilization must have awed Zhang, for while such an urban population did not rival that of Chinese cities in scale, the Han had believed themselves an island among seas of barbarians. This would challenge Chinese understanding of the world and their place within it – and, to the later cost of Dayuan, drove the Han to seek new ways to prosper through this recognition.

In his later report to the emperor, Zhang shared that the horses of Dayuan 'sweat blood and come from the stock' of the Heavenly Horses.[6] (This sweating of blood perhaps owed to a type of parasite feeding off the horses.) With the Han eager for allies and horses, this item in Zhang's narrative, quite incidental to his original mission, wound up being instrumental for the war with the Xiongnu and Zhang's standing in the court and posterity.

Though travelworn and lacking the splendid gifts with which he had left China a decade earlier, Zhang nevertheless presented himself to the king.

With Dayuan heavily invested in trade, Zhang must have been delighted to learn that the kingdom was aware of China and hearing of its great wealth, had sought to communicate with it, though so far without success. For realizing that Dayuan, at the southwest of Xiongnu territory, opened the Xiongnu flank, the *chanyu* might have actively blocked that communication between Dayuan and Han. The lands to the west of the Xiongnu represented a lifeline to them in their bruising clash with the Han and, surely, they meant to prevent that coming under threat – though they eventually could not stop it.

Zhang's arrival perhaps changed the king of Dayuan's calculations of his state's positioning and vulnerability. The Xiongnu exerted influence throughout the region and some buffer against them might have been most welcome. Or the king could have feared being caught in the vice between two empires, rather than simply manoeuvring against one. In any event, Zhang explained to the king his mission to contact the Yuezhi, promising if he provided guides to reach them 'and if I should succeed in reaching that country, on my return to China, my king will reward yours with untold treasure'.[7] The king acceded to this request and with these guides Zhang (and presumably Ganfu) departed Dayuan, travelling to the Syr-Darya River in Trans-Oxiana, known also as Sogdiana (a region now touching modern Uzbekistan, Tajikistan, and other neighbouring nations).

Along the riverbanks lived the nomadic Kangju people. Their lands stretched across modern Tashkent, Uzbekistan and some parts of Kazakhstan, and they paid tribute to the Xiongnu, whom they would directly support in coming battles in the region. They agreed to escort Zhang to the object of his search, carrying on through the final stretch to the domain of the Yuezhi in Bactria.

At long last he made contact with the people, for which he had trekked countless miles over trackless wastes and lived through captivity, not having seen his homeland for more than a decade. But all those privations would be worth it if he could convince the Yuezhi to align with the great power of a strengthening China in what would inevitably evolve into a mighty alliance.

Except the Yuezhi declined.

The Han had convinced themselves that they would have a great ally in the Yuezhi, or at least a barbarian mass they could steer to their purposes. Weakened by clashes with the Xiongnu starting in Chanyu Touman's time at the tail end of the third century BC, the Yuezhi were finally displaced by them circa 177 BC (it was then that their ruler's skull became Chanyu Modun's drinking cup). After this, the ruler's son and heir moved his people to Bactria. The Yuezhi unsurprisingly had scant appetite for abandoning their sweet and fertile lands to mount horses and string bows for war.

Zhang spent a year with the Yuezhi. Enough potential to forge some form of alliance or deal must have been mooted about for him to linger so long there. Perhaps he identified with a pro-war faction. Or perhaps he was not too keen to return to the Han and report on the utter failure of his mission. Despite what must have been desperate entreaties, he could not sway his hosts. However, unknown to him, he did lay some of the first stones of a path which would, more than a century later, lead to an alliance between Zhang's people and theirs.

Undoubtedly with a heavy heart and wondering how to frame this turn of events to the emperor – were he ever to make it back to court – Zhang began his return journey circa 127 BC. He followed a southern route, travelling by the Qilian Mountains range – near Qinghai, land of the restive Qiang tribes. But along these twisting paths, calamity struck: once again the Xiongnu captured him.

In some ways this period of captivity is even more mysterious than the first, for the context was very different from before. Now war raged between the empires, the marriage alliance providing no fig leaf of civil relations any longer. Multiple campaigns by both sides had led to huge numbers of war dead. However, in this instance, Zhang's time with the Xiongnu coincided with the death of Chanyu Junchen and the upheaval this wrought, with the *chanyu*'s younger brother, Yizhixie, and son, Yudan, each clawing for the throne, Yizhixie ultimately winning that struggle. Perhaps the Chinese diplomat, his acumen sharpened by ten years living among the Xiongnu, might have exploited this political chaos to his own ends. In any event, by unknown means he made good his escape, then tramped eastward circa 126 BC, finally setting foot again in the capital Chang'an. He returned to a transformed China, one that had been exploring the possibility of war at the time of his departure but was still locked in with the Xiongnu through the marriage alliance. Now it launched multiple expeditionary campaigns and as Zhang would later discover, needed officers to command the armies.

The report he gave on his travels, and later the strategy he outlined, profoundly changed the course of the war. While he failed at his principal object, he must have been able to embroider well on the other discoveries. For instance, the states to the west, Dayuan and Daxia (a kingdom in Bactria), offered commercial opportunity when Han would need infusions into coffers, particularly to replenish the war chest, and the support these kingdoms must have offered to the Xiongnu in trade and levies steadied their foe against Han depredations. A new front of the war would soon open. Zhang regaled Emperor Wu with tales of Dayuan, of Bactria and even farther west, the Parthian Empire. The wealth of these states – certainly as compared to the

Xiongnu and other peoples in China's periphery – made them an attractive market for Chinese goods and a source for new products in the Chinese marketplace. With the Han treasury depleted by the grinding war, this was a handsome development.

For the hardships he suffered and the valuable intelligence he delivered the court, in 123 BC Zhang received a fief and was granted the title 'Broad Vision Marquis'. But he did not linger long in the home he had for so long been absent from. Now his hard-earned knowledge could be brought to bear in combat.

From General to Private

After his diplomatic mission, Zhang's quixotic adventures continued as a general in the Han-Xiongnu War. Zhang had returned when there was a need for commanders in the field, and his experience in distant lands must have been seen as a unique edge in the fight. He was assigned under Wei Qing's command and would serve alongside Li Guang, each commanding his own unit. In 121 or 120 BC the two generals set out from Youbeiping in the northeast, Zhang commanding his own unit. The two units separated, intending a later rendezvous or perhaps to remain close enough for easy communication should one need to call on the other as reinforcement. Due to his travels and period living with the Xiongnu, Zhang's 'familiarity with the barbarian landscape, knowing where to find water and fodder, meant he could lead the army to these places and stave off thirst and hunger'.[8] Yet still he found himself lagging in the field.

Zhang undoubtedly lacked experience commanding a large unit in such complicated conditions as the steppe and desert. Li Guang's force of 4,000 cavalry fell into a trap, the Xiongnu encircling his force and laying waste to them. Whether after receiving word of the emergency or simply making his way to the rendezvous at an assigned time, nonetheless Zhang failed to arrive before Li Guang had lost a great deal of his men. Just as Li Guang would face censure one year later for his failed rendezvous in the Battle of the Northern Desert, now Zhang did.

Upon his return to China, he was sentenced to death. Further paralleling Li Guang in the aftermath of his 129 BC campaign fiasco, Zhang managed to save himself by paying a hefty fine and surrendering his noble status, his social rank knocked down to commoner, his army rank reduced to private. In the space of a few years he had plummeted from a hero to an embarrassment.

Zhang's Redemption

After narrowly avoiding execution, Zhang was motivated to return to the court's good graces and regain his standing. With the loss of the Hexi Corridor due to the Hunye king's defection to the Han, now the Xiongnu grew vulnerable. Yet this vulnerability and dwindling numbers, ironically, made the enemy more scattered and remote. Zhang, knowing the need for horses and allies, and drawing on information gathered in his original Yuezhi expedition, made a new proposal to the emperor:

> Now the [*chanyu*] has recently been defeated by China, in consequence of which the [Hunye king's] territory has become deserted; and since the barbarians covet the rich products of China, this is an opportune time to bribe the Wu-sun with liberal presents, and to invite them farther east in the old [Hunye] territory.[9]

The Wusun people, though a major group in the region, were not described in great detail by Chinese chronicles. As Indo-Europeans, their look might have been a shock to many Chinese, with reddish hair and other Caucasian features. Zhang's report suggests they followed similar customs to the Xiongnu – most likely their lifestyle also being one of nomadic pastoralism. After the Yuezhi clashed with the Xiongnu and withdrew in defeat circa 174 BC, the Yuezhi in turn pushed the Wusun farther west until occupying the Ili River Valley, an area northwest of the Tarim Basin. Forced into vassalage by the Xiongnu, over time the Wusun strengthened, with tens of thousands of warriors, enabling them to drift away from their overlords and spurn the summons to pay tribute to the *chanyu* at his Dragon Fort court. From these developments Zhang devised a strategy in which the Wusun could be turned against the Xiongnu. He further recommended to Emperor Wu:

> Should they become attached to the Chinese as a brother nation by intermarriage, the situation would be in favour of their listening to our proposition, and if they do this, it would be tantamount to the cutting off of the right [ie western] arm of the [Xiongnu] nation. Once we are connected with the Wu-sun, the countries to the west of them might be invited to come to us as outer subjects.[10]

'Cutting off the right arm of the Xiongnu' became something of a stock phrase, oft repeated in documents regarding Han strategy. The right arm was the support of the Tarim Basin states as well as the prospect of an alliance of the Xiongnu with the Qiang people in Qinghai. Zhang correctly analyzed that so long as the Xiongnu found support in allies, they could maintain themselves in opposition to the Han.

The possibility of an alliance with the Wusun must have washed away much of the emperor's disappointment following the Yuezhi's unwillingness to lend their might to the Han cause, and he set Zhang at the head of this new embassy. His age is unknown but Zhang must have been at least in his late forties. In 117 BC the expedition set out. This was around twenty-three years since he first departed on his mission to the Yuezhi. The emperor richly outfitted the expedition, this time with 300 men and huge numbers of livestock to sustain them en route. The grand, multiple objectives of the expedition also meant that many junior envoys accompanied Zhang. To bribe and bedazzle, and otherwise smooth his path, he carried great quantities of silk, gold, and other valuables.

The expedition traversed dangerous territory without any incidents reported in the records. Yet upon reaching the Wusun, their king, Kunmo, treated them in a high-handed manner. Perhaps it brought to mind Zhang's frustration with the Yuezhi, and he angrily retorted, 'If the king does not pay due respect to these gifts, which have come from the Son of Heaven, they will be withdrawn'.[11]

Any number of reasons might have laid behind Kunmo's behaviour, but possibly he was being watched by Xiongnu minders. The Wusun were likely wracked by internal strife and fearful of their former overlords, so wished to risk no immediate action. Open warfare had existed between the Han and Xiongnu for about fifteen years now; although the Han had scored some battle victories, and indeed, had greatly strengthened their position with the Hunye king's surrender, they struggled to consummate these gains strategically. The Xiongnu had already proven themselves powerful enough that they consigned the Wusun to vassalage. Thus the Wusun, as many others in this region did and would, found themselves trapped between the poles of two mighty powers, uncertain who would be ultimate victor but often asked to declare allegiance to a single side.

At this time the Wusun operated rather in the dark, as the great distance to China meant they knew virtually nothing of its power and wealth. Thus the wisdom of delaying commitment to Zhang at this point, for were the Wusun to enter an alliance with the Han, surely the Xiongnu would retaliate. Even granting Han forces safe passage might incur serious costs.

The chilly reception of Zhang's embassy must have filled Zhang with unease. These people were the key to his redemption in the eyes of the court and he had staked all his political capital with the emperor on success. Not abandoning hope, Zhang negotiated for the Wusun to provide guides for some of his expedition to travel onward to the west. Later, those guides paid a visit to China – likely in a stage-managed fashion – and upon their return, they told of its might and magnificent wealth. This was enough to tip them out of their indecision. At long last, the Han's quest for allies among the nomads was fulfilled.

This coup fuelled the restoration of Zhang's status with the court. He earned the title 'Great Traveller' in 115 BC and became a state minister recognized as an unrivalled expert in foreign affairs. Zhang could not enjoy his hard-won accolades for long, though, as he died circa 114 BC. Yet his legacy transformed China and the focus of the war against the Xiongnu.

China Looks West

As part of his projection of imperial majesty and to buttress his cult of personality, one of the pleasure gardens Emperor Wu had constructed in Chang'an was the lavish, finely manicured Shanglin Park. In it he displayed many treasures that had flowed to him throughout his reign, as seized war booty or as tribute from vassal states. Jade and other riches from Central Asia had pride of place, a shining manifestation of China's pivot towards the west which Zhang Qian had pioneered.

Zhang's adventures fuelled a new vision for China and brought about two intertwined policy directives: exploiting the commercial possibilities in western expansionism. Trade within China was hampered by its geography, with complicated north-south travel restricting the easy traffic of goods. But with the Hexi Corridor, western trade became quite viable, and the emperor and China became smitten with the rare goods to be found in lands which had been all but unknown before Zhang reported on them. And in this enterprise his name lived on, for 'envoys proceeding to the West after him always referred to [Zhang Qian] as an introduction in foreign countries, the mention of his name being regarded as a guarantee of good faith'.[12] A new commercial and potentially hegemonic vista opened before the Han – what would come to be known as the Silk Road.

The newly mapped strategic landscape also brought new thinking to the military. 'Cutting off the right arm of the Xiongnu' drove future objectives. Confronting the equestrian empire in the next phase of the war demanded operating in lands where the Han army had never marched before and squeezing value out of the promising new alliance with the Wusun. First, though, the alliance must be sealed through marriage to a Chinese princess.

Chapter IX

Princess Jieyou (d. 49 BC): Peace Bride and Han Operative

Their name meant 'Grandsons of the Raven' and the mystique this conjures can suggest some of the mystery surrounding the Wusun people. Like their former overlords the Xiongnu, the Wusun people frustrate the search for firm facts. Beyond their Indo-European roots, little has come to light of their language, religion, or other cultural practices. But to the Han, who in their annals became the accidental custodians of the Wusun in posterity, the foreign people's lands were rich and their horse stocks bountiful, and such details were sufficient.

Zhang Qian's report to Emperor Wu on his wide-ranging travels shared the legend of the Wusun and the tale behind their name:

> The king of the Wusun is known as the *kunmo*. The Wusun had lived to the west of the Xiongnu. When the Yuezhi attacked, they slew the *kunmo*. After his birth, the *kunmo*'s son lived in the wild, fed by a raven who brought him meat, and nursed by a she-wolf. The *chanyu* of the Xiongnu made the boy his ward, trained him and made him a distinguished leader of warriors.[1]

Mixing myth and probable history, the tale goes that, at the *chanyu*'s direction, the young *kunmo* returns to his people and serves as an affiliated king of the Xiongnu confederacy. The *kunmo* later received the *chanyu*'s blessing to avenge his father's death on the Yuezhi, whom the Xiongnu had recently (circa 177 BC) driven off. The Wusun launched a fresh attack, further displacing the Yuezhi and then settling in their territory. Buoyed by this victory, the *kunmo* increasingly resisted the Xiongnu yoke, refusing to report when summoned by the *chanyu*. This proved an alluring opportunity for the Han and the Son of Heaven sent them a letter:

> If the [Wusun] are able to move east and dwell in their former lands, then Han will send a princess to be [the king's] wife, and a fraternal alliance will be formed; we will together stand against the [Xiongnu] who will not be hard to defeat.[2]

Catching wind of this potentially catastrophic development, the Xiongnu began preparing a punitive strike against the Wusun. This in turn stirred the *kunmo*, Liejiaomi, to push through their partnership with the Han. They pledged 1,000 horses to their newfound ally, while China dispatched a young woman to cross the wilderness and wed the elderly Wusun king.

From Palaces to Walls of Felt

The woman chosen for this unfortunate honour, Liu Xijun (d. 101 BC), was the grandniece of Emperor Wu. Yet the crimes of her parents blemished that pedigree. Her father, a Han prince, somehow outraged the court enough to earn his execution, and her mother soon followed. So she fit the marriage-alliance mould well, being highborn yet also tainted. Political exigency would catapult her from a disgraced woman to a princess.

Sometime between 110 and 105 BC, Liu set off to be joined with her husband. She did not travel lightly:

> The presents included imperial carriages, wearing apparel and equipment for imperial use. There was established for her an official staff, and a complement of several hundred eunuchs and serving attendants and she was sent off with a very rich store of gifts.[3]

As she traversed the punishing terrain, the Chinese perception of the Wusun perhaps weighed heavily in her thoughts: 'The people are hard-hearted and greedy; they are unreliable and much given to robbery.'[4]

On arrival to her new people, buildings were constructed for Liu's use but in the meantime she would live in a nomad's tent. Wusun daily life remains opaque but in steppe societies women appeared to be prominent. With the rigours of the nomadic way of life and modest populations, drastically constraining women's contributions was untenable.

This struck a profound contrast with China, where women served under the rule of their fathers and brothers, husbands and sons. Though she lived in a later era of the Han dynasty, Ban Zhao (AD 45–115 – sister of the general Ban Chao, the subject of Chapter XIII) hints at the realities of most women's lives. While she contributed to a major work of history, the *Book of Han*, one of the classics of the Chinese canon and a testament to her deft scholarship, she also completed a primer for the comportment of young women, *Lessons for Women*. The following illustrates its tone:

A woman should be always humble and yielding. She should think of others always before herself. If she does a good deed, she ought not to publicize it, but if she errs, she must not deny it. She should endure disgrace as well as slander and actions against her. Always she should display a sense of fear.[5]

Raised with such strictures, Liu Xijun must therefore have been shocked by Wusun ways. Her contact with her husband appears to have been meagre:

> Once or twice a year she had a meeting with the K'un-mo, when a banquet was set out, and she presented the noblemen who attended the king with valuables and silk. The K'un-mo was old, and [he and the princess] had no verbal communication.[6]

Apart from those couple of days each year, hers was an existence most likely filled with longing and boredom. A poem attributed to Liu, recorded in the *Book of Han*, speaks to her state:

> My family sent me to wed the Wusun king
> A tent is my home, the walls made of felt
> I eat only meat, drink only sour milk
> My heart aches with longing for my own land
> And makes me wish I could as a swan fly home.

That is a testimony of the costs borne by these alliances which men like Zhang Qian were never asked to pay. To the Han, one woman's misery was a trifling price to pay, of course, for the alliance with the Wusun was of inestimable value to China.

In his final days the *kunmo* proposed to divorce Liu. This would allow his grandson and heir to marry her, maintaining the Wusun alliance with the Han. Here her discomfort with Wusun tradition reached fever pitch, as Chinese custom typically forbade widows to remarry. A horrified Liu appealed for relief from her grand-uncle Emperor Wu. 'Now that you are married to Wusun, you should accept their custom', he replied. 'I am most remorseful that you have to bear this demeaning and abominable arrangement to allow our kingdom to form an alliance with Wusun to fight against the Xiongnu.'[7] After Liejiaomi's death (circa 104 BC) she married his successor Junxumi and gave birth to a daughter. Then her suffering reached an end, for she died shortly after. The Han would need to replace her, but there were other disgraced women to choose from. And this one certainly would not display a sense of fear.

Princess Jieyou (d. 49 BC): Peace Bride and Han Operative

A Different Kind of Warrior

Zhang Qian achieved far more against the Xiongnu as a diplomat rather than a lackadaisical general. To build on his success, and to score blows against the resilient enemy, individuals with other talents must step forward, women like Princess Jieyou. Like Liu Xijun, Jieyou bore a taint which spanned generations, for her grandfather, the King of Chu, had been one of the architects of 154 BC's Rebellion of the Seven States and died by his own hand following its failure. As such, she was a prime replacement for her predecessor.

Upon arriving to take up her post and marrying Kunmo Junxumi circa 104 BC, Jieyou found she would share her husband with a Xiongnu princess. Though the Han had a treaty with the Wusun, the Wusun were not prepared to close off possibilities and also held an alliance with the Xiongnu. Each an agent of their respective empire, the two women sought to bind the Wusun ever tighter with their people while no doubt sabotaging the relationship of the other. In the early period of Jieyou's tenure, though, the Xiongnu were losing ground in this unusual contest. Before Junxumi's death (circa 93 BC), he named his cousin Wengguimi – known to the Chinese as the 'Fat King' – as his heir. Over the coming years Jieyou and Wengguimi had two daughters and three sons.

In choosing his cousin, Junxumi had passed over Nimi, his son with his Xiongnu wife, as the boy was deemed too young to serve the office. However, upon reaching his majority he would become king, and then with a half-Xiongnu ruler, China's enemy would gain significant influence. Surely this preyed on Jieyou and the Han's courts thinking, but in the meantime the Xiongnu already exerted pressure on their former vassals and insisted the Wusun end their alliance with the Han. As a figure of high position in Wusun society, Jieyou served as a sort of intelligence officer. Around 75 BC, she dispatched a letter alerting the court that the Xiongnu had assembled its forces with the intent to fall on the Wusun and claiming that 'only the Son of Heaven is in a position to save' her adopted people.[8]

The appeal moved the emperor and he ordered a campaign in response. But his death in 74 BC halted the momentum. Despite this Han inaction, no major Xiongnu attack seemed to land. Perhaps it had all been a Xiongnu ruse, or Jieyou had misread the situation, or the attempted Xiongnu action miscarried, though they did execute a number of smaller-scale attacks, even capturing territory, which Jieyou reported to the new emperor Xuan (92–49/48 BC, reigned 74–49/48 BC):

The [Xiongnu] have time and again sent out large forces to penetrate and attack ... They have sent envoys ordering [the Wusun] to bring the princess [Jieyou] with all speed, and they wish [the Wusun] to sever relations with Han. The [king] is willing to put half the state's best troops in the field; he will himself produce 50,000 cavalry, men and horses, and will exert his strength to the utmost to attack the [Xiongnu]. It rests only with the Son of Heaven to send out a force so as to save the princess and the [Wusun].⁹

This time the emperor saw the action through. In 71 BC the Han dispatched 150,000 troops and together with the Wusun's 50,000, the allied army crushed the Xiongnu force. The alliance so long pursued by the Chinese had faced a trial by fire and passed with aplomb.

Marriage as Battleground

In 64 BC, Kunmo Wengguimi, showing how effectively Jieyou fused marital and political affairs, contacted the Han court stating his intention to monumentally alter the balance of power in the region. He planned to make Yuanguimi, his son with Jieyou, his heir and to sever Wusun's ties with the Xiongnu. If the Han might send a princess for Yuanguimi to marry, they could seal these new terms. For Jieyou, this would truly be a family affair – her niece was selected as the peace bride.

Now someone with Chinese blood in their veins would rule the Wusun, and the Han must have envisaged tremendous gains for their cause. Instead, they would stomach grim disappointment. After the young woman departed with a delegation, word came that Kunmo Wengguimi had died. Rather than acting on Wengguimi's wish to confirm Yuanguimi, the Wusun nobles instead brought Nimi to power. At China's westernmost city of Dunhuang, the Han delegation lingered while one of the officers escorting the princess rode ahead to the Wusun. He upbraided them and asked them to recant, but to no avail, and the princess returned to the capital. But despite this snub the Han could not afford to lose influence on their ally, especially as with a half-Xiongnu king at the head it would surely drift deeper into the Xiongnu sphere. Jieyou married Nimi, son of her original Xiongnu rival. Despite their no-doubt stormy relationship, the two had a son together.

Sometime later, a Han delegation arrived on routine business. Jieyou reported to her compatriots that her husband 'was a source of distress and suffering to the Wusun and could be easily punished'.¹⁰ Her precise role in what followed remains cloudy but can be guessed. A banquet was laid for the visiting dignitaries. Whether or not at Jieyou's signal, one of the Han soldiers rushed Nimi, drew his sword and struck the *kunmo*. Yet it was not a mortal blow and Nimi fled out of the tent, mounted a horse and escaped into the night. Nimi's son assembled troops and surrounded Jieyou and the others until a Han relief force arrived, scattering them.

Again in an awkward spot with the Wusun, the Han hastened to patch up the shaky partnership. Another delegation arrived, delivering medicine for Kunmo Nimi's wounds and presenting gifts of gold and silk to him. The officer leading the delegation arrested two of the prior Han party's leaders and beheaded them. Suspicion then turned to Jieyou – had she overstepped her authority and masterminded this assassination attempt? Though in his interrogation the officer clutched her painfully by the hair, Jieyou strenuously denied her guilt and was ultimately found innocent. Not one to endure such insult, she later reported her mistreatment in a testimonial to the court and her interrogator was executed.

Though Jieyou – if indeed she was a conspirator – had failed to kill her husband, Wusun intrigues would finish the job. Wujiutu, son of Wengguimi and a Xiongnu mother, fled at the time of the attack and formed a coalition of Wusun and Xiongnu followers, killed Nimi, then claimed the *kunmo* title. Unsettled by these developments, the Han sent out an army to put Wujiutu down. But here Jieyou and one of her handmaidens, Feng Liao, brought their talents and experience with the Wusun to bear. Feng Liao, known as Lady Feng, had married a Wusun prince who was a trusted friend of the usurping *kunmo*. Dispatched by Jieyou to Wujiutu, Lady Feng convinced him to stand down, otherwise the Han would crush him.

Lady Feng then travelled to the emperor, where in a personal audience she weighed in on the matter. The result was that Wujiutu would accept a reduction in rank to 'Junior King' while Yuanguimi would be 'Senior King'. Jieyou and Lady Feng's energetic diplomacy forestalled open war and ensured continuing Han influence in Wusun affairs, deepened by a half-Chinese *kunmo* now in power.

The decades came and went. Both Jieyou's son Yuanguimi the Senior King and her other son by Nimi preceded her in death. Jieyou

> sent a written report to the effect that she was old and her thoughts were with her homeland, and that she would like to be able to bring her bones back for burial in Han territory. The emperor felt pity for her and had her fetched, and she arrived at the capital city in company with her three grandchildren.[11]

Nearly seventy, she returned to China in 51 BC. In her two remaining years she appeared at court and received many imperial gifts, recognition that in her decades of service she had transformed the dynamics of the western region, which was fast becoming a crucial theatre of the Han-Xiongnu War.

Chapter X

Li Guangli (d. 88 BC): Hunter of Heavenly Horses

The alliance with the Wusun first brokered by Zhang Qian and later solidified by Princess Jieyou yielded much advantage to the Chinese, from striking fear into the Xiongnu to accessing desperately needed horses. The Wusun maintained their own herds and provided mounts to their new partners. At first, it seemed the occult had even weighed in on the matter:

> Sometime earlier the emperor had divined by the *Book of Changes* and been told that 'divine horses are due to appear from the northwest.' When the Wusun came with their horses, which were of an excellent breed, he named them 'heavenly horses.'[1]

(As we shall see, the emperor's use of divination and belief in witchcraft would play another, darker part in this story.)

Yet when the emperor reviewed some horses from Dayuan – those that Zhang Qian noted would sweat blood – he found them markedly superior. Forthwith the Wusun horses lost their august title and the Dayuan horses, bred strong and healthy in their wholesome valleys, claimed that moniker. Yet what did it matter if the swelling Han herds kept horses of first and second ranks along with the lower-quality horses bred in Chinese territory? The demand for horseflesh was keen, and the emperor bid an embassy bearing 1,000 gold pieces and a golden statue of a horse to travel to Dayuan and purchase as much of their herd as possible.

Dayuan, however, did not wish to do business with China, frequently hiding their horses when buyers came seeking to obtain them. The Han believed the finest steeds were being kept hidden in Ershi, the capital city known also as Sutrishna. Dayuan surmised that supporting the Chinese by selling their horses could put themselves in peril of Xiongnu retaliation. And they did not fear spurning China:

> The Han lies a vast distance from us. Many times they have suffered and died while attempting to cross the salty wastes which lie between us. To

the north, should the Han attempt it, the Xiongnu await them. To the south, the lack of water and pasture will cause them misery. And with the lands they must traverse holding few towns, they will find little resupply. When their parties do arrive, even if only originating as a few hundred men, more than half die en route. Given all this, do you truly believe they could send an army here?[2]

Instead, Dayuan reserved its fear for the nearer and better-known Xiongnu. Yet Dayuan misjudged the Han, their lust for horseflesh, and the extent to which they could mobilize to gain control of a wealthy and vitally strategic region. China's lack remained so pressing, the government in 103 BC appropriated civilian horses (surely ill-suited for warfare) into the army.

Zhang's report on Dayuan ignited keen interest. The distant kingdom could serve as a springboard to launch explorers in the Zhang vein even farther west, and by pulling the kingdom into the Han orbit, the Chinese might gain control of a Xiongnu flank. Perhaps it would even be as easy as Dayuan recognizing the magnificence of Chinese civilization and simply agreeing to vassalage.

But when the Chinese embassy bearing the golden statue arrived it was met with contempt. Whether the Han representatives caused insult or not, they were rebuffed, the goodwill Zhang seemed to have earned with Dayuan seemingly gone. In a fit of pique the Han envoys destroyed the horse statue with a hammer and made for home. The incensed Dayuan rulers commanded Yucheng, one of their cities on the eastern border, to block the embassy from reaching China.

Envoys can play an instrumental role in foreign relations, as agents of power projection, brokers of commercial links, and collectors of intelligence. In this instance, they gave their lives and thus became a *casus belli*, for soldiers from Yucheng intercepted and slew them.

The envoys served as representatives of the emperor and through their murder Dayuan had committed an outrage against the sanctity of the Dragon Throne. News of it injected hot blood into otherwise-cold geopolitical calculations. Dayuan must now be brought to heel and pay for its crime. In turn this would announce to all the states and peoples of the region that they would be wise to fear the Han more than the Xiongnu, however near the nomadic empire might lurk. Emperor Wu, though his empire was strained by fighting the Xiongnu, now pursued a new foe in what would come to be known as the War of the Heavenly Horses. He merely needed the right man for the job, and he chose Li Guangli.

Trekking to Dayuan

Unlike many of the generals preceding him, such as Wei Qing, Li Guangli (no relation to Li Guang) did not come from the frontier region but instead the Zhongshan ('Central Mountains') region in central China. Much like Wei Qing, though, Li's star rose through the beauty of his sister, a favoured concubine of Emperor Wu. This made Li something akin to the emperor's brother-in-law and meant privilege and access. Perhaps more critically, it also meant imperial forbearance when he failed, which few other Chinese subjects could rely upon.

There is not a great deal recorded about Li's military record prior to his selection as general for the campaign against Dayuan. This might suggest there was nothing for Sima Qian to note, or only an embarrassing record (it must be remembered that, when writing of these contemporary events, Sima acted at the pleasure of Emperor Wu, one of the most powerful men in the world). In any event, whether he possessed a deep well of military prowess and experience or not, as an intimate of the emperor Li Guangli received high rank and command of an army. Perhaps drunk on recent Han successes, such as the Battle of Mobei, and wishing to show favour to his favourite concubine, Emperor Wu ennobled her family through her elder brother. Even before he set out, he was gilded with unearned honours, in a fit of monumental hubris: 'With the expectation that he would subdue Ershi and seize its uncommon horses, Li Guangli received the title Ershi General.'[3] The tradition of naming a conquering general after the place he conquered is widely accepted, but typically conquest must actually occur first.

The hubris escalated. Around that time the Han erected Shou Xiang Cheng, the 'City for Receiving Surrender', along the border. Experts contended Dayuan would easily fall to Han military might, with past envoys assuring the emperor a force of 3,000 crossbow-armed soldiers could take the upstart city.

While Li did not march out with quite so few men, the assessment of Dayuan's strength still played into the assembling of a trifling Han force. In 104 BC Li Guangli set forth with 6,000 horsemen drawn from area vassals and allies. Undoubtedly these forces served as the backbone of the campaign, although, while the horsemen might have been effective on the battlefield, likely their loyalties and level of commitment did not equal their abilities. Malcontents conscripted from across the empire, numbering 20–30,000, deemed unfit for service in the Xiongnu theatre but suitable for action against feeble Dayuan, rounded out the ranks. All in all, few might mistake this for a cohesive, professional force.

This motley army marched past Lop Nor, the Salt Swamp. One of the critical challenges of campaigning in these lands was obtaining food. Supply chains would be next to impossible to maintain and living off the arid land an impossibility for such a large army – precisely why Dayuan had dismissed the Han as a military threat. Evidently Li Guangli planned to take provisions along the way from friendly or cowed peoples. However, when his army approached the denizens of the smaller Dayuan cities, they retreated behind their stout walls. Unlike the Xiongnu, these urbanized people embraced fortifications. Quickly it became plain that the nature of combat on this campaign radically diverged from the lessons learned in the field fighting nomads.

Han doctrine had developed toward engaging a specific type of foe, mounted archers rather than hardened positions, and the army needed to retrain and retool. Now siegecraft would come into play, warfare based on patiently waiting out foes while constructing and deploying siege engines. In some ways this played to Chinese strengths, suited to their traditional forms of combat, with fighting focused on static targets rather than a fluid foe. It is likely that laying sieges played a part in the 154 BC Rebellion of the Seven States and certainly in earlier days of intra-Chinese warfare.

At the same time, if obtaining food challenged the army on the move, when stationary for longer periods, as sieges demanded, its soldiers would grow all the more hungry. Forage in this landscape would have been extremely limited. Though perhaps there existed fertile, well-irrigated pockets, these would only sustain an army for so long, and only in some seasons.

Li's army attacked the fortified Dayuan cities he encountered, but they held fast against the Han aggression. Some attacks succeeded, with the Han breaching the city or accepting surrender, which granted a fresh supply of provisions. But other siege attempts failed, the Han army dropping the operation after several days and marching on. These failures to force the submission of cities – undoubtedly smaller and weaker than sturdier ones in Dayuan such as Ershi – must have given pause to Li Guangli, or at least to sober-minded officers in his command.

Harsh conditions, compounded by the scant provisions, ground away at General Li's force, more damaging than combat. 'Thus by the time Li Guangli reached Yucheng he had no more than a few thousand soldiers left, and all of these were suffering from hunger and exhaustion'[4] – hardly suitable conditions to take on Yucheng, surely a stronger foe than those faced previously. Yet Yucheng had the blood of Han envoys on its hands; to restore Chinese honour, punishment must be meted out. With Li bogged down and investing various cities on the way (it took two years for the army to reach Dayuan), Yucheng had ample warning to brace for a siege, laying in provisions, bolstering fortifications, and calling in levies and allies – perhaps even from the Xiongnu.

Undeterred, the general who already bore the title of an even-greater city's conqueror went on the attack. As to be expected, Li was easily repulsed, taking enormous casualties. Now the demoralized general faced an awkward choice: if even Yucheng, at the east of the Dayuan domain, could withstand them, what chance had he to cross hostile Dayuan territory and then attack Ershi, the capital, no doubt even more formidable than all other cities they had encountered? So instead, licking his wounds, Li retreated to the border city of Dunhuang. When he arrived with his army, they were reduced to between ten and twenty per cent of their starting strength.

Li sent a letter to the emperor apprising him of the military situation. In short order he received simple imperial guidance in return: anyone from his army caught venturing deeper into China would face summary execution. Holed up in the stifling heat of a Dunhuang summer, General Li was trapped in a choice between more feckless campaigning or imperial fury if he travelled homeward. Probably only his sister's relationship with the emperor saved him from a death sentence.

Meanwhile, another calamity struck the Han. In a separate campaign in 103 BC, the Xiongnu encircled an entire army commanded by Zhao Ponu (whose name, ironically, meant 'Crush the Xiongnu Slaves') and captured 20,000 Han troops.

Emperor Wu's advisors urged that Li Guangli's army rush to seal the gap, that Han forces quit what they now called the 'Western Territories' and concentrate on direct action against the Xiongnu. Decades of war had already drained the imperial treasury – could the Han truly afford war on multiple fronts? The pressure mounted to break off the disastrous Dayuan campaign.

The emperor, however, would not accede to this – should the Wusun, the Yuezhi, Daxia, and other nations of that region witness the Han failing to take Dayuan, the Chinese would be seen as a paper tiger. Its stake in the region, which promised new streams of wealth and a fixed target at which to strike the Xiongnu, stood in jeopardy. Emperor Wu also still raged about the killing of his envoys by Yucheng and demanded this affront be avenged. Though the decision likely contravened the guidance of many advisors in the civil service, this moral rationale surely stiffened Emperor Wu's resolve in supporting the wild gamble Li Guangli would make for him.

Another Stab at Dayuan

The Han held an almost-insuperable advantage over their Xiongnu enemy. While the quality might be lacking, they could always draft more men into the struggle. First, in response to the recent capture of the 20,000 troops by the

Xiongnu, Emperor Wu directed an incredible 180,000 men to take station at Jiuquan ('Wine Spring'), reinforcing the border and discouraging the Xiongnu from further aggressions. That settled for now, he turned to Li's misbegotten campaign. Seeing that Li's original force lacked crushing numbers, the emperor threw open the gates of his prisons and poured convicts into the campaign, pardoning them and massing a giant army of 60,000 to reinforce it.

In addition to what must have been an infusion of low-quality troops, a few specialists also joined. Anticipating the seizure of the famed horses, he sent master horse breeders along. Based on some intelligence about the city's water sources, experts in hydro-engineering were assigned as well, and they would play a key role in the siege. Newfound Han allies the Wusun, called by Emperor Wu to join the campaign, dispatched 2,000 horsemen. Finally, 50 commanders reported to General Li; one wonders if they were meant to ginger up their general and keep him on track.

From Dunhuang the giant army marched out in 102 BC. While on their way to Dayuan, the cities that ignored and resisted Li two years earlier now piled supplies and honours on him. Though one city, Luntou, defied him and refused to submit. Over many days Li's army laid siege to it, and after the city weakened, he launched a massive assault which at last breached the city's defenses. Li gave the soldiers leave to sack Luntou and massacre the residents. For General Li, this barbarity delivered twin benefits: it relieved some pressure on his army by allowing his beleaguered men to vent their frustrations, and among other cities in the region, word spread of the sacking, hastening their cooperation and surrender as the army marched onward.

Attacking Yucheng, the city that had slain the Han envoys and thereby helped provoke this war, was initially an objective, but General Li opted against this. He reasoned that becoming bogged down in a siege there would only afford Dayuan's capital Ershi more time to reinforce itself. So his army carried on its advance. General Li led a reconnaissance in force, commanding the vanguard with 30,000 troops, and upon approaching the city made contact with the Dayuan army. Under a withering barrage of Chinese missile fire these defenders crumpled, falling back to the fortress city of Ershi. The Han momentum faltered, though, when the Wusun warriors refused to fight, unwilling to risk offending the Xiongnu; in a sign of the complicated politics of the region, the Wusun sought not to provoke the steppe empire which might still prevail in this theatre.

Ershi maintained outer and inner walls, and must have been nearly impregnable. Scouts from Kangju, aligned with the Xiongnu and an ally of Dayuan, appeared to observe the siege. They rode back to report to their masters to help decide whether Kangju might come to Dayuan's aid.

For forty days Li Guangli besieged the mighty city. Perhaps the most powerful asset in their arsenal was not the siege engines or catapults, but the intelligence which had prompted the hydro-engineers to join the campaign: Ershi was watered not by wells shielded by the city walls, but by rivers flowing into the city. At last a chink in Ershi's defences might be attacked. Damming and diverting the water, the Han specialists parched the city. Anticipating the siege, the inhabitants surely had massive stores of food, but soon they would know terrible thirst.

The opposition against them weakening, the Han now landed a heavy blow when they breached the outer wall and captured a famed noble of the city. At this the defenders and inhabitants fled within their inner wall. While they might have continued to resist effectively, without an adequate supply of water they must have recognized the severity of their plight and some of the nobles began to conspire:

> The killing of the Han envoys and the hiding of the horses by our king invited this attack upon us. We can find our way out of this predicament by assassinating the king and surrendering the horses to the Han. Surely that will prompt them to then take leave of us peacefully. But if they persist in their siege, we shall fight to the last man. And soon, perhaps, Kangju will ride to our aid.[5]

The faction of conspiring nobles promptly executed their king. Bearing his head as a token of their sincerity, a Dayuan emissary visited Li Guangli, promising that if the siege were lifted, the general may select the finest horses in the Dayuan herds. Should the general refuse, they would slaughter the horses, denying the Han the primary objective of their campaign.

Despite the king's execution and a potential deal with the city nobles, the outcome of the siege still hung in the balance. 'Word has come to me,' Li Guangli shared with his officers, 'that there are Chinese within the city skilled at digging wells'.[6] Knowing the tenacity of the Dayuan defenders, this surely represented a serious threat to Han success. He also noted that the inhabitants still possessed adequate food supplies. Now that the stalwart Dayuan king had been slain, Li observed:

> If under these circumstances we refuse to withdraw our troops, the inhabitants will defend the city to the last man. Meanwhile the scouts from Kangju, seeing our soldiers wearied by the siege, will come with troops to rescue Dayuan and the defeat of our army will be inevitable.[7]

Thus General Li agreed to the emissary's proposal and the famed blood-sweating horses were trotted out for inspection. The master horse breeders which accompanied the campaign made their selections, taking more than 3,000. Before departing, the Han also installed a noble friendly to the Chinese as the king of Dayuan, making a tractable client of this once-proud and independent city-state.

The army began its march home. The Xiongnu, no doubt inflamed at Dayuan being clawed into the Chinese sphere of influence, coordinated with the kingdom of Loulan – a place of huge significance in the coming years of the war – and dispatched soldiers to engage the withdrawing Han army. Yet they arrived too late and missed their chance.

The Han victory at Ershi did not hold across Dayuan, however. On the return march, Li split his forces, and one unit's route took them past Yucheng. Perhaps flush with the memory of their recent success, though only 1,000-men strong, the Han unit moved on the city and invested it. Three thousand soldiers of the Yucheng garrison burst out and cut them apart.

Upon learning of this disaster from survivors who caught up with him, Li Guangli ordered one of his officers to ride back in force and subdue Yucheng. When this unit approached, the Yucheng king saw the impossibility of resistance and fled to Kangju for sanctuary. Again illustrating the complexities of foreign relations here, the Xiongnu-affiliated Kangju nevertheless delivered him to Han justice. The king who had ordered Emperor Wu's envoys with the golden horse put to death was executed.

In the spring of 101 BC, Li Guangli returned to China to report his mission accomplished to his brother-in-law. The emperor likely harboured mixed feelings about Li after the general's retreat from the first attempt to take Dayuan, and his poor leadership allowed for officers' neglect of their soldiers to result in grievous losses. Still, the objective had been met; Li had fulfilled the ambitions of Zhang Qian, and securing a Chinese toehold in Central Asia and establishing a puppet state held tremendous promise. Li Guangli was duly rewarded, enfeoffed as a marquis and, despite his spotty record, the emperor assigned him a new task and a new foe.

Campaigns Against the Xiongnu

After the oblique strike against the Xiongnu sphere of influence by attacking Dayuan, it came time for a more direct action. His faith in Li Guangli restored, in 99 BC Emperor Wu placed General Li in command of 30,000 cavalry. At the head of this force Li launched from Jiuquan to engage the Sage King of the Right, who protected the western territory of the Xiongnu, and his forces situated around Tian Shan (the 'Celestial Mountains'). It would prove a campaign of disastrous turns but also of valour under fire.

The Battle of the Celestial Mountains

Details are thin on General Li's actions, but initially he met with success, his army slaying or capturing 10,000 Xiongnu. The mission accomplished, they turned and began the journey back to the safety of their own lines. But then another Xiongnu force swooped in and engaged them, surrounding the army. Han casualties mounted and the army could find no means of escape.

There is no record of cunning or brave actions by Li, but two of his subordinates distinguished themselves. Rather than simply digging in and repelling an onslaught, one officer, Zhao Chongguo, opted for a brazen charge on the enemy. Leading 100 cavalrymen, he sallied forth, boldly cutting a swathe through the Xiongnu, enabling General Li and his army to break out. This time, the general kept his good name.

Li Ling and Sima Qian

A sub-general in Li Guangli's campaign had a historic encounter with the enemy and as a result, profoundly affected the life of his friend Sima Qian, author of *The Records of the Grand Historian*, the major primary source for the Han-Xiongnu War and much else. Li Ling (no relation to Li Guangli, though he was the grandson of the general Li Guang) had joined the campaign despite a lack of horses, persuading the emperor that he had developed infantry tactics which could compensate for that shortcoming. With 5,000 men, whom he assured the emperor were master swordsmen from the south of China (an area famed for its swordplay), he marched in a separate unit from Li Guangli.

Li Ling's novel tactics faced a clarifying test when he encountered an overwhelming Xiongnu mounted force. It proved a miniaturized version of Wei Qing's Battle of the Northern Desert, though with a rather different outcome. Despite vastly outnumbering the Chinese, Xiongnu overconfidence sent their horsemen into volleys of disciplined crossbow fire, and after the enemy regrouped, Li Ling ringed his wagons to form a defensive perimeter (through some contorted logic he also executed women and children who had followed the soldiers in a bid to tighten their focus and raise morale). By maintaining cohesion and exploiting terrain to the utmost, he kept his unit on the move, repulsing Xiongnu charges all the while. But the superior numbers eventually told against him, and the lack of resupply sealed his fate. When their crossbow bolts ran out, his force was quickly overrun, only 400 of his 5,000 men escaping. In despair Li Ling surrendered to the enemy.

Despite killing many Xiongnu soldiers in the engagement, Li Ling found a warm reception among them. The *chanyu*, Qiedihou (d. 96 BC), gave him his own daughter in marriage. Li Ling lived out the rest of his days among his former foes. But back at court, his name was blackened with accusations of treason, Emperor Wu apoplectic at the defection. Alone among the emperor's ministers and advisors, Sima Qian spoke up in defence of Li Ling. For this loyalty to his friend he suffered terribly. Sentenced to death by Emperor Wu, Sima Qian was offered a commutation of this punishment, one to which many preferred death: 'getting sent to the "silkworm house"', or castration (itself often a death sentence, with many recipients of the surgery dying in agony in the aftermath). Yet the call of his unfinished work on his opus *The Records of the Grand Historian* steeled Sima Qian for his choice. After surviving the surgery, he continued writing and eventually even returned to the court to serve the emperor who had ordered his mutilation. In a letter to a friend, Sima Qian shared what drove him to carry on.

> Yet the brave man does not necessarily die for honour, while even the coward may fulfil his duty. Each takes a different way to exert himself. Though I might be weak and cowardly and seek shamelessly to prolong my life, yet I know full well the difference between what course ought to be followed and what rejected. How could I bring myself to sink into the shame of ropes and bonds? If even the lowest slave and scullion maid can bear to commit suicide, why should one like myself not be able to do what has to be done? But the reason I have not refused to bear these ills and have continued to live, dwelling in vileness and disgrace without taking my leave, is that I grieve that I have things in my heart which I have not been able to express fully, and I am shamed to think that after I am gone my writings will not be known to posterity.[8]

Despite the pain and indignities he suffered, Sima Qian continued writing his grand work of Chinese history, including recording the twisted end of Li Guangli.

Black Magic

The next several years of Li Guangli's life were spottily recorded. In 97 BC he rode out at the head of a massive force in search of Chanyu Qiedihou. Not desiring a pitched battle with a numerically superior army, the Xiongnu retreated, denying contact but later fighting a small engagement. The campaign lacked distinction for Li, and soon he withdrew for home.

In 90 BC General Li again took the field at the emperor's order. As he rode out of Chang'an with his army, the Han chancellor, whose son had married Li's daughter, saw him off. Standing at a bridge, Li shared his hopes that the son of his sister and the emperor might be made crown prince, and then departed. He never saw Chang'an or his family again.

Later, while marching out of the Shuofang Commandery near the border, Li's mighty forces of 60,000 cavalry and 100,000 infantry came to a sudden halt at the discovery of a hobbled Xiongnu warhorse in their path. Obviously meant to be found, it sent some form of message to the Han or invoked spirits against them. Geomancers were rapidly summoned to make an assessment; after their procedures, they claimed the signs for a triumphant campaign remained auspicious.

Curses and hexes abounded in this time, often roiling the Han court. Factions perpetuating their intrigues found accusations of witchcraft against enemies a potent weapon, sometimes resulting in the alleged perpetrators' entire families being annihilated. Unfortunately for Han military operations, these frenzies could reach all the way to the top.

This was a stormy time for the emperor. In 91 BC his son, the Crown Prince Liu Ju (nephew of the celebrated Wei Qing), had been framed by court enemies on charges of witchcraft. This forced the prince into an impossible position: likely his best chance at saving his life and those of his family would be through mounting a rebellion. Yet when he attempted this, it quickly miscarried and ended in his suicide, followed by the murder of his two sons by Han soldiers. Against this backdrop of probable guilt and madness, shyster shamans and soothsayers repeatedly hoodwinked Emperor Wu. He sank deeper into the occult, had lately been suffering recurring nightmares, and at this stage of his life he may well have been senile. The emperor was now an unstable, dangerous element in the empire, as Li would shortly discover.

As the general penetrated farther north, Xiongnu scouts reported the approach to their *chanyu*, Hulugu (d. 85 BC). Hulugu withdrew and chose his preferred battleground near the Yuwu River, where he and ten thousand cavalrymen unleashed their assault when the Han army came into sight. This opened a ten-day battle with Li and his army largely on the run. In the midst of this Li captured a Xiongnu and from him learned that the hobbled horse encountered early on the march was not an inconsequential message but in fact laid a curse on the Han army. But it was not this curse which was Li's undoing.

In the hysteria of the witchcraft scare at the Han court, perhaps compounded by Emperor Wu's senility, Li Guangli's son fell under suspicion as a culprit. The Han chancellor, Li's relation by marriage, was also arrested, then paraded in a pig cart before being publicly executed; his wife soon followed. While in the field Li received word of this and feared for his family. One of his secretaries subtly suggested he defect to the Xiongnu rather than return to his homeland. Li considered such a course but decided instead to drive onward. If only he could inflict a massive defeat on the Xiongnu in their territory, Li would earn such plaudits from the emperor that it would clear his family's name. So, rather than racing back to his family's defence, Li ordered his army ever onward. He dispatched an officer with a force of 20,000 to cross a river and engage the Xiongnu, resulting in a bloody day of fighting. Troubles mounted: he faced a mutiny, the mutineers alleging the general had lost his nerve and vigour. Li put down the attempt, though, and executed the ringleader.

Then word came that Li's family had been liquidated.

Throughout the long war, Han imperial paranoia and totalitarianism drove loyal men into the enemy's arms. Devastated – and likely questioning loyalty to a regime which had senselessly murdered his bloodline – the general and his army surrendered to the Xiongnu. Yet, as with Li Ling before him, the Xiongnu magnanimously welcomed Li Guangli into their fold. In fact, the *chanyu* wed his daughter to Li and showed him great honour. In a cruel twist, while Li Guangli, haunted by the murder of his family, made a new life among the Xiongnu, allegations of witchcraft would continue to torment him, for superstition was an effective weapon in both societies. He fell afoul of Wei Lu, a Han official who had defected to the Xiongnu and now grew jealous of the attention the *chanyu* paid Li. Wei concocted a dangerous calumny against him.

The *chanyu*'s mother having fallen ill, Wei Lu suborned a shaman to pinpoint a supernatural cause for her illness. The shaman demanded of the *chanyu*, 'We had vowed prior to each campaign that if we were to capture Li Guangli alive we would have him sacrificed. Why have you recanted?'[9]

The *chanyu* saw wisdom in this. Li Guangli was seized, his hands bound, and he was placed on a sacrificial altar. Before his throat was slit, Li Guangli laid his own curse upon his killers: 'When I am dead, my spirit will return to annihilate all you Xiongnu.'[10]

It is unknown whether the *chanyu*'s mother recovered from her illness.

Death of the Martial Emperor

In 87 BC the death of Emperor Wu, who had loomed so profoundly over the course of the war with the Xiongnu, at last ended his 54-year reign. Time and again his ironclad commitment to prosecuting war meant it carried on even in the face of military, financial, and societal catastrophe. Yet the war was now so ingrained in Han culture, even his death would not shake the Han following that course, especially as fissures widened among their longstanding enemy.

Chapter XI

The *Chanyus* Zhizhi (d. 36 BC) and Huhanye (d. 31 BC): A Broken Brotherhood

In a break from the precedent of his imperial predecessors, Emperor Wu, from the outset of his reign, embraced a vigorously hostile posture against the Xiongnu. In the wake of his death, the hammer blows of Chinese expeditionary campaigns did not land with the same force or frequency. They did not need to, for the Han had become indisputably the superior force.

The successes achieved during Emperor Wu's reign, such as reclaiming the Ordos Plateau region circa 127 BC, the defection of the Hunye king in 121 BC, the circa 116 BC alliance with the Wusun, and the continuing projection of power into Dayuan and the Western Territories, meant the need for striking at the heart of the Xiongnu faded in urgency. The war had also cost the imperial treasury dearly. These factors, combined with the emperor growing more aged, meant the Han could adopt a lower-intensity stance. If fighting must be done, better to let barbarian vassals handle it. China could hunker behind the Great Wall and leave its troops garrisoned at the border, mostly to man their stations rather than to embark on sorties and expeditions. Campaigns into the northern wastes cost the treasury dizzying sums, when there were victories they were not lasting, and calamity always loomed. In this time of strength and stability for the Han, why take such risks?

Ironically – though perhaps surmised by Han war planners – this somewhat aloof stance posed danger to Xiongnu integrity. They required an external force to galvanize them; denied that, the vast differences and grievances among the many tribes of the confederacy could grow too salient. Turmoil would soon find them, brother turning on brother.

Compounding Crises

While the advent of the Han following the Qin collapse did spell a more organized adversary to the Xiongnu, it also offered opportunity. Fractious tribes could set aside their grievances and unite around a common enemy and common source of wealth and glory – and under a unitary leader, the *chanyu*. A China struggling to overcome its age-old divisions and meld as a single state would also pay handsomely to be left unmolested so it could concentrate on that gargantuan enterprise.

Ever since Zhang Qian blazed the trail, the Han's continuing involvement in the Western Territories threatened the Xiongnu. Li Guangli's costly but successful campaign against Dayuan, with the Han installing a client king, put the Western Territories in the awkward position of being flanked by the Chinese while the Xiongnu lurked at their northwest edge – a state of affairs the city-states of the Tarim Basin found vexing to navigate. With the defeat of Dayuan, many city-states opted to pay tribute to the Han and tilt into their sphere of influence. This was a dramatic reversal from the days when Han envoys had been disdained as interlopers, ripe for fleecing, while 'whenever a Xiongnu envoy appeared in the region carrying credentials from the *Shanyu*, he was escorted from state to state and provided with food, and no one dared to detain him or cause him any difficulty.'[1]

The Western Territories presented the Han with a static target which allowed them to hack at the underbelly of the otherwise-evasive Xiongnu. The city-state of Jushi (near modern Turpan in Xinjiang Uyghur Autonomous Region, China), an ally or client of the Xiongnu, became the focus of much fighting. It was strategically essential for the Han because of its centrality in the corridor for western communication, and for the Xiongnu because it provided much of their sustenance. The Han had developed a military farming system, called *tuntian*, which made army units far more self-sufficient, growing their own crops while also denying pasturage to the enemy's horse and other livestock herds. Xiongnu raiders targeted these farms, and eventually they drove off the Han workers, though no one was left to run the farms and they soon went fallow.

Even as the Xiongnu scored minor successes, they lost the shield of their reputation, and when it was challenged, they lacked the manpower to punish the upstarts. Local rivals nibbled at Xiongnu flanks and increasingly engaged in provocations. Circa 78 BC members of the Wuhuan people (formerly of the Donghu 'Eastern Barbarians', the confederation destroyed by the Xiongnu *chanyu* Modun) vandalized *chanyu* tombs. They had been made vassals of the Xiongnu following that defeat. Prestige was fundamental to maintaining power and for the Xiongnu it was beginning to sag. And due to Zhang Qian's diplomatic efforts, the Wusun had of course gone over to the Han. When the Han did take the field against the Xiongnu, they did so with these new allies. Circa 71 BC, after Princess Jieyou reported Xiongnu war preparations of the Xiongnu to the Han court, a massive army set out supported by the Wusun king, Kunmo, and 50,000 of his riders. They tore deep into Xiongnu territory, attacking the lands of the Sage King of the Right, capturing or killing 40,000, including many commanders and members of royalty.

That winter, the Xiongnu sought to avenge this outrage from their former vassals and rode against the Wusun. But a curse seemed to cling to them. They only managed to capture civilians and, far worse, on their return trip a blizzard hit. Between this and other misfortunes, only ten per cent of the army survived the ill-starred campaign. Now the Xiongnu were beset on all sides, with the Dingling tribes of Siberia pushing south against them, the Wuhuan in the east, and Han and Wusun also pressing. They suffered combat deaths but surely far more from the livestock seized by their attackers. Yet the gravest danger lay within the heart of Xiongnu society itself.

The Xiongnu Civil War

Since the inception of the Xiongnu, their political structure seemed to rest on wobbly ground. A patchwork of varying linguistic, ethnic groups without a clear ideology and spiritual underpinning, their commonality at the least deepened through the danger they shared in the Chinese.

The *chanyus'* mode of succession also entrenched the potential for instability. With brothers of a deceased *chanyu* potentially valid candidates, well-established royals with powerful followings could vie for the throne. In this regard, the Xiongnu power structure comes off as gesturing toward something vaguely democratic compared to the stultifying certainty of Han succession, as subjects could exercise more autonomy in choosing who they supported. Projecting influence, rewarding allies with treasure and their own prestige which gained them standing from their own constituent tribes – these qualities made a Xiongnu leader. Yet this reality could invite recklessness and chaos with multiple contenders seeking to rule, and an inability to cohere in a fashion capable of withstanding profound shocks to the body politic. Exogenous shocks from Han military aggression only intensified this.

When in 60 BC Chanyu Xuluquanqu died, a lasting political order monopolized by a single lineage of the Luanti clan, an undivided Xiongnu nation ruled by ten generations of leaders, died with him. A man of a rival lineage claimed the throne and then consolidated power by installing friendly individuals to key offices throughout the confederacy. This provocative action provoked the ire of the lower rungs of society. The *chanyu* was deposed but without a clear choice to fill the absence; in the ensuing free-for-all many noble Xiongnu with sufficient masses of followers made a play for the throne; 57 BC saw five nobles of various lineages declaring themselves *chanyu*, including

Huhanye, son of Xuluquanqu. The following year, his elder brother Zhizhi asserted himself as the leader.

As camps coalesced around each brother, the Xiongnu empire effectively partitioned into spheres centred in the north, ruled by Zhizhi, and in the south, ruled by Huhanye. Zhizhi held an advantage militarily, being a superior general and commanding a significantly larger army. In 54 BC he drove Huhanye from his occupation of the Xiongnu capital at Dragon Fort. Conditions for victory, or even mere survival, quickly soured for Huhanye. So he considered turning to an unlikely ally.

Submission to the Han

> By no means! It is the character of the [Xiongnu] to value independence and disparage submission. By mounting our horses and fighting for the national cause, we have gained renown for courage among all nations whose sturdy warriors fight to the death. Now we have brothers striving for supremacy, and if the elder is successful it falls to the younger. Although both may die in the contest, they leave an unsullied reputation for courage to their children and descendants, excelling all other nations. Although China is strong there is no reason why the [Xiongnu] should be annexed to it.[2]

Thus did one of Huhanye's advisors rail against the proposal under consideration, of surrendering to the enemy they had been fighting for decades and had once held in their grasp. It was not succumbing to the Han which they most feared or reviled, but to other Xiongnu. Living with the Han might be more palatable than living under Zhizhi.

Debate was fierce though. 'Our Kingdom was founded on horseback and warfare; our motto is to wage relentless battles,' observed another, and later added:

> Han is a mighty kingdom – much as they have tried they have not been able to subjugate us. Why do we have to be disloyal to our ancestors and founding fathers by disrupting our established custom? If we were to surrender, it would be the greatest insult to our ancestors.[3]

Yet the founding fathers of the Xiongnu lived when their power peaked and the Han trembled at the drum of their horses' charging hooves. This was a different age; the realists made a painful but persuasive case. One of these replied:

We have to face the reality that we do not have the resources to recover what we have lost. I know we are unyielding and resilient however under the present circumstances we have not seen peace for a long time ... we are destined to be annihilated if we choose to continue along the present path. The reality is plain for all to see, no other plan is more pragmatic.[4]

This advisor who pushed for submission to the Han won the day.

Huhanye sent his son to the Han as a token of his submission. Then, in 52 BC Huhanye entered the passes and proffered himself. A Han mounted force escorted him to Chang'an, the roads lined with 2,000 additional cavalrymen. On the first day of the lunar new year he called on the court, though the homage he offered was meagre, essentially token, so the slight on his dignity was minor. His position – hotly debated by the emperor's counsellors – was placed above other vassals, as a visiting head of state.

While Xiongnu leaders had submitted before, such as the Hunye king in 121 BC, for the Han a *chanyu* represented an earthshaking triumph. The long-suspended marriage alliance provided the political foundation for this, a model both sides could look to. For the Han, friendly Xiongnu at the border meant dramatically reducing the expense of maintaining security, resources which could instead be used toward other priorities, such as consolidating their grip on the Western Territories.

Huhanye moved his people south, settling close to the Chinese 'City for Receiving Surrender' and the Han provided them grain and other necessities. The emperor personally showered treasures upon Huhanye but the priceless gift – though a poisoned chalice, perhaps, for both parties – was Han support in his peoples' affairs. With Chinese financial and military backing, Huhanye and his Xiongnu faction could rewrite their geographic, demographic, and political conditions and, newly strengthened, confront his brother and rival, Chanyu Zhizhi, despite his more substantial forces.

Zhizhi Fights On

At a stroke Huhanye's submission profoundly altered the dynamics of the region, beginning the inclination toward the Han as the regional locus of power. Understanding China's might, many states of the Western Territories, those kingdoms caught between the two poles of titanic empires, followed suit and swallowed their status as vassals.

Zhizhi still tried salvaging the situation for his people, to bring the Han to the bargaining table, but with Huhanye's Xiongnu faction in the Han's pocket, it served multiple Han purposes to keep one bloc in favour and one out. This accorded nicely with the Chinese doctrine of 'barbarians fighting barbarians' and could sow lasting discord among literal brothers – all to the good, by Han reckoning.

Now Zhizhi was surrounded by the Wusun, the Southern Xiongnu augmented with Han materiel and reinforcements, the Dingling to the north and the Wuhuan in the east. The Wusun attempted to lure Zhizhi into a trap, but the wily *chanyu* sniffed it out and put his attackers to flight. In 51 BC the Dingling launched an assault but again his response drove them off. Internal challengers also came at his throne. In 49 BC one such would-be *chanyu* rallied his men, prompting Zhizhi to meet him in battle. The *chanyu* defeated him, claiming the upstart's 50,000 horsemen to buttress his own strength.

More struggle awaited. In 48 BC famine swept the land and the Han sent emergency rations to Huhanye to see his people through it. With the Han backing Huhanye with foodstuffs, military aid and more, Zhizhi's prospect of unifying the Xiongnu through conquest winnowed to an ever-more-slender reed. Zhizhi scrambled for some way to alleviate his people's suffering, dispatching his son as a hostage to the Han court, hoping this gesture might open negotiations with them.

It was not to be. Zhizhi's son was rejected as a hostage by Chang'an. When he returned to his father, a Han court official accompanied him. An unknown incident during this exchange set off Zhizhi and in his rage he had the official executed.

No doubt anticipating blowback, Zhizhi strayed west, far from the Han. He focused on rebuilding his power through that once-dependable source of Xiongnu support, the city-states of the Tarim Basin. Soon envoys from Kangju, whose lands Zhang Qian visited, appeared. Kangju had been resisting encroachment by the Wusun and hoped to enter an alliance with Zhizhi against them. The Wusun were a hated enemy, a Han ally that had caused havoc for the Xiongnu people, and Zhizhi happily established his people in the eastern domain of Kangju. An exchange of Zhizhi's and the Kangju king's daughters as wives cemented the alliance.

Merging his forces with Kangju's, in 44 BC Zhizhi took the fight to the Wusun, the combined army killing and capturing their people and herds as well as threatening their capital. Zhizhi was fast becoming a major threat to their expanding hegemony of the Western Territories. Not only was Wusun now the Han's critical ally, a linchpin to Chinese ambitions in the region, but their crown prince had a Han mother through the marriage alliance, and thus held promise down the line of more fundamental Chinese control of these people. The Chinese could not dismiss Zhizhi's aggression against their ally.

Despite their early joint military success, over time the Xiongnu-Kangju relationship soured, the reasons not indicated but possibly what happened next suggests Zhizhi's volatile anger played some part. Thrown into a rage by something unrecorded, Zhizhi slew his wife, daughter of Kangju's king, and then 'slaughtered several hundred Kangju nobles and civilians; he then ordered to have their remains dismembered' and tossed into a river.[5] The despotic *chanyu* then pressed the people of Kangju to toil on a mighty structure, 'Chanyu Fortress'. It likely stood near a river, its rampart formed from rammed earth, the inner structures made of wood.

Later, Han envoys located him and demanded the remains of the official Zhizhi had murdered. To this the *chanyu* sent the mocking message, 'I am in an impoverished and appalling state. I intend to surrender to the great Han Kingdom.'[6]

Soon the Chinese answered this provocation.

The Battle of Zhizhi

At this time, the Han court was ever more involved in the minutiae of military operations, and rapid deployments in reaction to dynamic opportunities often fizzled while a reply from the bureaucrats was in transit. Confucianism, with its suspicion of military action, gained even more currency in the court. A man of the army hungry for advancement faced a challenging landscape.

Chen Tang, a Han officer eager to make his name, had been dispatched to the region in 36 BC. Attempting to persuade his superior officer, Gan Yanshou, to take decisive action against Zhizhi, the superior waffled, insisting on first seeking permission from the court. Chen advised Gan to avoid this protracted step by simply taking the decision unilaterally. Gan demurred from such a brazen act but when he later became ill, Chen seized his chance, forging Gan's signature authorizing a levy of troops drawn from area vassal states. Before Gan could halt the mobilization, 40,000 men responded to the call. Zhizhi's tyranny also won him enemies among the Kangju. Two of its nobles and their followers joined Chen in his brewing campaign, sharing intelligence on the strengths and layout of the *chanyu*'s redoubt.

With these combined forces and vital information at their disposal, the unruly officers Chen and Gan advanced on Zhizhi's fortress. By chance, a Kangju force, returning from raids against the Wusun, encountered the baggage train of the Han army and plundered it. Upon hearing of this, Chen dispatched his men after the Kangju warriors and slew them, though perhaps some of them slipped away and gave warning to Zhizhi.

When he learned of the host closing on him, Zhizhi understood the enormity of his peril, that a broad coalition of states had united to destroy him. He also believed the king of Kangju would not stand by him through the battle, so he made an unusual choice for a Xiongnu commander: rather than go out and meet his foes in the field, he dug in. It is interesting that the *chanyu* opted to fight from a static position like this, as he had already proven himself a successful commander in the field, using the trademark Xiongnu mobility for overwhelming strikes. Most likely the Xiongnu did not excel at sieges and had virtually no experience defending against them. Still, perhaps Zhizhi lacked the numbers to take on such a large force, or the Kangju troops now represented a core part of his army and their unreliability made open battle with them too great a risk.

Zhizhi dispatched an envoy demanding the intent of the closing army. The response: since Zhizhi had told the emperor he wished to surrender, this army would happily escort him. Further, they added,

> We have travelled long distances, our men and horses are exhausted, our supplies are running low and we are extremely concerned that we might not even make it back to our capital. Your Majesty, please send a senior minister to confer with us.[7]

Such mockery must have set off the irascible *chanyu*.

From his battlements manned by several hundred soldiers, Zhizhi watched the Han fortify its perimeter with a palisade. He ordered 100 heavy cavalry and an equal number of infantry to sally out. They charged the palisade, only to lose their nerve upon seeing the crossbowmen arranged behind their secure vantages, and the attackers instead reeled back to the fortress as the Han archers pelted them with missile volleys.

Swiftly a frontal assault followed in which the Han set the wooden walls ablaze. Still the fortress held. That night some Xiongnu attempted escape, only to be felled by Han projectiles. From the battlements, Zhizhi rallied his soldiers, among which now numbered his wives and concubines. He fought on until an arrow or bolt struck him glancingly on the nose, forcing him back within. That night the Han won through the outer wall, forcing the defenders to withdraw.

Zhizhi could only brace for the inevitable end. But then, a chance at survival glimmered: 10,000 Kanju troops arrived at last to aid the besieged. Zhizhi must have felt his hopes soar as he watched them assault his attackers. But almost as quickly as they delivered Zhizhi hope, it turned to ashes. The Han palisades and other defences were proof against the Kangju charges, and the would-be relief force melted away.

With attention no longer divided the attackers set fire to the palace, flames spreading through the night. Han war drums pounded and horns blared as the besiegers edged closer, their combat engineers raising great earthen ramps to storm the fortress. Zhizhi retreated to his inner palace with 100 of his men, but his end was written. The Han forces breached the final defences and emerged with Zhizhi's head as a trophy. This marked a momentous military achievement: the first Xiongnu *chanyu* to die in battle fighting the Han.

Spoils of Capitulation

The grisly end of Zhizhi, with his head presented to the emperor and put on display, likely had multiple effects on his brother Huhanye. With Zhizhi no longer presenting a threat to the Chinese, his faction broken for the time being, perhaps Huhanye wondered if the Han saw diminishing returns in maintaining him. This encouraged him to solidify the relationship. In 33 BC he travelled to Chang'an to reaffirm his submission to the empire and asked to be considered Emperor Yuan's son-in-law. Wang Zhaojun, an imperial concubine and legendary beauty, joined the *chanyu*'s stable of wives. For the purposes of this political exchange, she was considered an ersatz daughter of the emperor.

In gratitude, Huhanye wrote to Emperor Yuan that he would safeguard the sanctity of China's border and therefore, why not pull the Han soldiers from their garrisons and allow them to go home? Surely this would give him and his people more breathing room, and perhaps increase his standing, seeming less a pawn of the Han.

After vigorous debate, the Han emperor, though initially leaning towards agreement, decided against Huhanye's proposal. The potential threat of a reinvigorated Xiongnu state always loomed. And the continuing need to prevent disaffected Han subjects escaping to the north, possibly to involve Xiongnu in their intrigues against the Chinese imperium, remained alive to the policymakers.

Huhanye, the *chanyu* who gave the Han what they had long pined for, died in 31 BC. His alliance with China ushered in decades of good relations with the Xiongnu. Huhanye's queen declared:

> Our Kingdom has suffered from more than ten years of internal strife and natural disasters, the destiny of our people was hanging by a thread and we barely managed to persevere, much of that was because of the Han Kingdom, which helped us scrape through our most wanting years.[8]

In the coming decades, though, the Han would see the strength and vitality that had brought a large Xiongnu faction under their power ebb and all but vanish.

Part Four

Warriors at the Imperial Sunset

Chapter XII

King Xian of Yarkand (d. circa AD 62): Han Ally Gone Rogue

The Han dynasty fell in AD 9 but it was not the Xiongnu who toppled it. Though many factors worked against the regime's integrity, weakening leadership played a telling part. After the death of Emperor Wu, the Han did not seat a successor with the vision, energy, and importantly, the longevity to ever match his. Many of the late Han emperors did not survive even into adulthood, a persistent problem which set the conditions for the Han's takeover by a usurper.

The Wang Mang Interregnum

The ever-expanding traffic into the court of concubines and consorts bred tangled admixtures of families who had touched imperial greatness. Relations of suddenly well-placed women now found themselves poised for true power. Clans plotted for their sisters and daughters to bear the next Son of Heaven and thereby lift their fortunes beyond measure, and they would conspire against one another, through poisonings, accusations of witchcraft, and other devious means to clear their paths. Against this backdrop emerged Wang Mang (45 BC–AD 23), member of a formidable clan, who manoeuvred into a position of influence as tutor to a young emperor. Soon he extended his grasp by becoming the boy's regent. When the emperor died, a mere infant – selected by Wang Mang – succeeded him. Without a strong presence on the Dragon Throne to resist his grasping, Wang faced no real challengers and in AD 9 seized the throne. The Han was out; in with the Xin ('New') dynasty.

Wang prided himself as a Confucian scholar; yet while Confucians prized good order, he immediately sowed chaos. Wang had an obsessive concern for re-enacting past glories, guided by ancient texts and practices which predated even the early Han era by centuries. The Xiongnu and their newfound standing with the Chinese challenged this vision. Alliances with Xiongnu made friendly to the Han – the legacy of Chanyu Huhanye's submission – did not square with Wang's Confucian stance. He had various official seals and titles granted them rescinded, cultivating enmity against him. The old pattern resumed of

Han soldiers defecting from China to the Xiongnu through disaffection or fear of persecution by the new regime.

The Western Territories, most of the kingdoms in the firm grip of the Chinese during the late Han period, responded angrily when Wang stripped their status as well. Nor did his dynasty make good on the compact formed under the Han – that China would protect its western allies from Xiongnu interference. In AD 13 the kingdom of Karashar (known as Yanqi by the Chinese) rebelled, slaying the Xin governor and thereby touching off an uprising throughout the region. The Han had been a force in the Western Territories for well over a century, but through a few quick blunders the Xin wiped out their predecessors' gains.

Wang's tumultuous rule, in which he insisted on consulting ancient sources to guide modern policy, and that he stood at the centre of nearly every substantial decision of a sprawling government, continued to encourage dissension and gave otherwise disconnected groups a shared enemy. Han loyalists made common cause with rebel peasant armies, such as the Red Eyebrows (named literally for painting their eyebrows red), who in AD 23 brought down the Xin dynasty. Storming Wang's palace, the people slew him, hacked his body to pieces and threw them in the street. A member of the Liu family line was set on the throne, a rickety Han dynasty restored under Emperor Gengshi. His reign name meant 'New Beginning' – fittingly, for this was not the Han of old.

Shaky Rise of The Eastern Han

The lineage of the Han rulers which began with Liu Bang and ran until Wang Mang's short-lived interregnum came to be known as the Western or Former Han, and this new period, the Eastern or Later Han. At first, it seemed a false dawn for the dynasty, as Gengshi's reign lasted a mere two years. His alliance with the Red Eyebrows soured when leaders of the peasant army went unrewarded with titles and domains, and they had the emperor strangled in AD 25. A rival relation of Gengshi was crowned as Emperor Guangwu later that year, establishing a modicum of stability at long last. Then began a period of new rulers striving for the energy and might of the Western Han but finding their authority primarily through their distant genetic links to the former royal family.

The choice of the Eastern Han capital city unmistakably signalled the nature of the new regime's priorities and capabilities. Rather than continuing to rule from Chang'an, Guangwu shifted the capital to Luoyang, about 400 kilometres (250 miles) to the east. Luoyang had briefly served as Liu Bang's seat of government but he had recognized the importance of a western vantage on his kingdom, perhaps from which he could better monitor and counteract the Xiongnu. Under the Eastern Han, no longer would the emperors draw vigour and influence from the frontier, but rather gain respectability from the literati and business interests of central China. Imperial authority waned and regional power bases rose up – a throwback to the early days of the Western Han, these localized polities diluting the strength and coordination of the empire. This resulted in massive enterprises, such as how the Han-Xiongnu War had been prosecuted from the Battle of Mayi in 133 BC to the 53 BC submission of Chanyu Huhanye, being all but entirely undermined. Now the focus skewed inward towards the domestic. In some ways, this emperor faced conditions similar to China's position more than two centuries earlier, when Liu Bang had no choice but to ignore threats and incursions from the north, so that he could concentrate his energies on cobbling together an empire and remain ever vigilant against internal threats to the fragile union.

The governing philosophy accelerated its drift from the austere, state-focused Legalism and embraced the rising tide of Confucianism, which promoted moral cultivation of the individual. Confucians mistrusted warfare and relations with those who did not respect its ingrained hierarchies between emperors and subjects. Peoples outside of China, of course, did not neatly conform to such pieties.

Whether out of political preference or, more likely, a lack of viable options, Wang Mang's retraction from the north and the west continued under Guangwu. The relocation of the capital also signalled what would be a profound change in China's dealings with the frontier and its peoples – essentially a resignation from confronting and managing the complex region. Wang Mang lost much ground, and China's decision, no doubt reluctant, to sacrifice any remaining position in the region left a vacuum. Withdrawing from the north and the west, shrinking the border regions of settlers, the Eastern Han adopted a purely defensive stance, creating the conditions for an enemy which had fought over generations to restore itself.

The Xiongnu Snatch an Opportunity

> Now a state of anarchy is present in China. Wang Mang has usurped the supreme power, thus when the [Xiongnu] also sent troops to attack him, devastating his border land, this caused great consternation throughout the empire and the thoughts of the people reverted to the Han. Wang Mang has been killed, his cause overthrown, and thus through our means the Han has been re-established. Now we ought to be treated with greater honours.[1]

This speech of Chanyu Huduershi (d. 46 AD) wonderfully underscores the depth of relationship between the Xiongnu and Chinese. According to this, the Xiongnu viewed their role as almost symbiotic, lending a hand to the Han so they can together sweep away the turmoil of the Xin dynasty interregnum, for a China at war with itself, with harvests missed and energies spent toward reforging a union rather than defending a stable empire from external threats, spoiled opportunities for the Xiongnu. Yet chaos in China also helped the Xiongnu find focus and, though still fragmented, to drive back into their former sphere of operations and influence.

The faction which had originally followed Huhanye, previously settled within or close to Han territory, now no longer under the watch of Chinese wardens, drifted back to the Hexi Corridor. This brought them into closer contact with their estranged brothers, those who had once followed Chanyu Zhizhi. Gradually these residual factions coalesced, strengthening under Huduershi's leadership. They struck out at rival groups in the region of what is now modern Mongolia, such as the Wuhuan, to assert their reviving power. After recapturing the Hexi Corridor, the Xiongnu began projecting power through it back into the Western Territories. Their hold on former client or vassal states tightened once again, the empire taxing them hard to replenish their shallow coffers. Rapidly the Xiongnu returned to health. When Emperor Genshi had invited them back to the marriage alliance system, the Xiongnu refused, saying they would no longer even nominally submit to the Han; instead, the Chinese should pay explicit homage to them.

The Han was a fading power, and the Xiongnu a rapidly regrowing one. Both sought the wealth and strategic value of the rich trading kingdoms of the Tarim Basin, but for now China could barely maintain its decayed presence there. Ultimately this settled into the main arena between the empires, the conflict shifting from a direct Han-Xiongnu contest to more of a proxy war. Those in the Western Territories had to walk a difficult line in this volatile period if they wished to avoid subjugation. Or they could exploit the profound turn in the political landscape and seize independence and power.

A King Charts His Own Path

Yarkand, known also as Shache and Suoju, was a city-state of the Tarim Basin whose strategic placement at the junction of the northern and southern branches of the Silk Road enriched it and made the tiny kingdom punch above its weight in the region. Formerly under Western Han control, it had proven a vital asset in the region enabling the Chinese to both expand and protect their trade. Yarkand's king, Yan, who had been a hostage of the Han when young and grew enamoured of the culture of his keepers, instituted Chinese-style rule at home and instilled admiration of the Chinese in his sons, Kang and Xian. When the Xiongnu returned to the Tarim Basin, Kang succeeded after his father's death in AD 18 and led his people to fend off being clawed into vassalage. For this Kang received Han plaudits and emblems of office recognizing him as an honoured ally. Upon Kang's death in AD 33, Kang's younger brother Xian stepped into the role.

Xian meant to immediately cut his own path. He attacked two nearby kingdoms and placed his nephews – his brother Kang's sons – as their rulers. Other kingdoms to the east fell under his sway. He was proving both a success on the battlefield and a great asset to the Han – as their nominal agent, he kept them a presence in the region, however attenuated now. In AD 41 he dispatched envoys to the court seeking recognition of his actions on behalf of – or at least to the advantage of – the Han. These services were duly recognized and seals and other symbols of his new title, 'Protector General of the Western Territories', were conveyed to the envoy for delivery to King Xian. Then something intruded on what promised to be a mutually advantageous relationship.

Whether out of a fussy sense of protocol, racism, or perhaps well-founded concern about a Han client proving too powerful, a Chinese administrator objected to Xian's status and his title was downgraded. This bureaucrat likely did not appreciate the stunted range of Han power projection. Better, most likely, to find ways to manage what remained of their deteriorated presence in the region; insulting their few remaining allies was not the means to achieve this. Despite the protests of King Xian's envoy, the seals and other tokens of the king's 'Protector General' rank were taken against his will. At a stroke, the Han, only beginning to vaguely resemble the reach and might of their imperial forebears, had burned a key ally in the region.

Cut off from Chinese support yet also freed from their demands and interference, King Xian continued blazing his own path. Weaker kingdoms he forced into submission. Stronger ones, like Kucha, a rich city-state generously watered by an oasis and placed by vital trade routes along the northern border of the Taklamakan Desert, he repeatedly attacked, though for now Kucha held fast against him. While he focused on consolidating his power, perhaps he could also punish the Han for their intransigence. Chinese trade still flowed through the region, capitalizing on the burgeoning Silk Road linking with the Tarim Basin, Bactria, Sogdiana and other nearer regions, all the way to the Parthian Empire and beyond.

Located around the marshes near the salt lake of Lop Nor, the city-state of Loulan (the Chinese rendering of Kroraina) offered little arable land but its position on the Silk Road made it vitally important to the Han. Loulan was a vital conduit of this commerce and one the Chinese had been involved with for more than a century. Due to its proximity to Yumen, the Jade Gate in the locale of Dunhuang which defined the western edge of Chinese territory, they could easily strike at it, with the commander Zhao Ponu capturing the kingdom in 108 BC. It then became a Chinese foothold in the Western Regions. With a tiny population, perhaps of 14,000, Loulan was a pawn between the Han and the Xiongnu, seeking to find a balance between superpowers, often hedging their bets by sending hostages to both empires. Even then their weak position meant little safety – a Loulan prince who had lived as such a guest of the Han was later condemned to existence as a eunuch for some unspecified infraction.

Its value to the Han obvious, in AD 46 Xian demanded Loulan block all Chinese traffic flowing west. The Loulan king refused and put the Yarkand envoy to death. Xian called up his army.

It was a rout, the Loulan king fleeing for his life. Xian installed a puppet ruler. Frequently he drew these leaders from other kingdoms and rotated them, both denying existing power bases and preventing them from cultivating new ones in their temporary assignments.

Concerned at King Xian's swelling dominion, unaligned kingdoms hastened to offer their sons as hostages to the Han in the hopes of protection. But the dynasty still struggled to gather itself and could not afford to extend protection so far from its core territory. Emboldened, Xian expanded his campaign. Loulan and seventeen other kingdoms offered tribute and their sons as surety of allegiance, beseeching help from the Han. Chinese trade must have suffered at this time, as after subduing Loulan Xian would impose the traffic blockage which had precipitated his attack in the first place. Here, with a bloc of kingdoms seeking help, came an opportunity the Western Han forebears salivated for: by granting their protection, the Chinese could solidify their footprint in the region.

This was a different time though. To these earnest entreaties the emperor replied: 'We are not able, at the moment, to send out envoys and Imperial troops so, in spite of their good wishes, each kingdom [should seek help], as they please, wherever they can, to the east, west, south, or north.'[2]

The kingdoms could not resist Xian on their own. So they did seek protection elsewhere, turning to the other power in the region.

Xian Resists the Xiongnu, Alone

Xian's rapidly spreading suzerainty meant he needed to stud the region with loyal power bases. Dominating the kingdom of Kucha, he set his own son Zeluo on the throne. But perhaps Xian had overextended himself. Resistance began to quicken against him, and the Kuchans rose up and put Zeluo to death. They then begged the Xiongnu for protection and received it in return for the Xiongnu making a shrewd selection of Kucha's next king, thus ensuring Kucha would remain firmly within their sphere.

Other kingdoms, including Dayuan, so expensively claimed by the Western Han through Li Guangli after the two campaigns of the War of the Heavenly Horses, fell to Xian. When kingdoms grew restive, or Xian simply suspected them of such, he summarily executed their leaders. But he ran into trouble with Khotan (known also as Yutian), another state which had grown rich from its quarrying and trade in jade. Ordering a general from another part of the region – Xian's standard method for selecting temporary tyrants – to keep the city-state under control, the newcomer soon earned the hatred of the locals. A Khotan noble assassinated the general with an eye toward claiming the throne, only to be murdered himself by another Khotan noble, Xiumo Ba, who rose to the kingship and pre-empted Yarkand retaliation by assassinating another of King Xian's generals stationed in Khotan.

A furious King Xian ordered an army of 20,000 to Khotan. Most likely Xian's levies lacked the heart for fighting to aid his ambitions and when Xiumo Ba engaged the Yarkand soldiers, he slew half their number. Xian took personal command and led another army assembled of men across multiple kingdoms to crush the rebel army. Once again, the Yarkand army suffered defeat and Xian fled for the safety of Yarkand, Xiumo Ba snapping at his heels.

The Khotanese laid siege to the city. It looked like this would be the end of Xian's tyranny – until Xiumo Ba took an arrow wound. The campaign against Yarkand could apparently not sustain itself without him, for at his death his army evaporated. Yet Xiumo Ba's nephew Guangde, affirmed by kingdoms allied to Khotan, assumed the crown and he strengthened himself – at least in the near term – by becoming a client or ally of the Xiongnu. Khotan's ranks filled out with Xiongnu veteran mounted archers, Guangde attacked Xian again but could not yank the king from his redoubt.

Though King Xian appeared safe so long as he clung to his walls, an armistice with Guangde would be preferable to gambling on further combat with troops who in recent clashes had poorly shown their mettle. In AD 60, to demonstrate the earnestness of his peace pledge, Xian released Guangde's father who had for many years been a prisoner in Yarkand. The king also presented his own daughter as a wife to Guangde. Hostilities soon cooled now that Yarkand and Khotan were united by family ties.

But the peace was short lived. In AD 61 Guangde raised an army of 30,000 and again attacked Yarkand. A baffled Xian dispatched an envoy to his son-in-law: 'I have given you your father and your wife. Why are you attacking me?'[3]

While impossible to know the factors leading to Guangde's aggression – and it may be as simple as a quest for power or to avenge the death of Xiumo Ba – perhaps the Khotan king's affiliation with the Xiongnu compelled him to attack. Guangde had first to draw Xian from his fortress, however. To his question Guangde replied, 'O king, you are the father of my wife. It has been a long time since we met. I want us to meet, each of us escorted by only two men, outside the town wall to make an alliance.'[4] This appeal to familial relations assuaged King Xian. Though he had pursued a career filled with violence and deception, he blithely departed for the rendezvous. Guangde seized him and a traitor within Yarkand threw open the city gates, enabling Khotanese soldiers in to capture Xian's family, including Xian's son Bujuzheng. King Xian was held prisoner in Khotan, only to be killed circa AD 62.

Somewhat confusingly, Guangde's actions, or his political designs in the aftermath of the victory, upset the Xiongnu. It suggests how warping the projection of Han and Xiongnu power into the region could be for the kingdoms and statelets striving for independence and stability. The Xiongnu raised forces from various client states and attacked Khotan, Guangde buying his life by offering tribute and his son as the bond of his loyalty. Later, the Xiongnu insisted Bujuzheng be placed on the Yarkand throne. In AD 86, Guangde attacked, slew Xian's son and installed his own son as king, ending generations of Xian's family line ruling the dark-horse state.

Chapter XIII

Ban Chao (AD 32–102): Wielder of Brush and Sword

At this very hour our fate is being decided. To die without glory is not the act of valiant men![1]

After delivering these words, Ban Chao led his thirty soldiers through the darkness outside the walls of Loulan. Though commanding only the security detail for a diplomatic delegation, he decided he must act on his own authority. The many tents of the encampment loomed ahead – the Chinese were quite outnumbered but at least the darkness cloaked them as they stalked nearer. And they had surprise. Ban noted the direction of the wind, instructed some of the soldiers to ready their torches, and positioned his crossbowmen.

At long last, the Han would strike back at the Xiongnu in the Western Territories, and Ban would earn his place in history.

Raised Among Literati

The Eastern Han period were uncertain days for an army career. Philosophies espoused by government officials in tandem with desperate economic and political conditions conjured strong headwinds against military development and action in the Eastern Han period. Confucianism, an ever-more-deeply rooted political and social philosophy in Chinese life, promoted its distaste for militarism, perhaps exemplified by the adage, 'nails are not fashioned from good iron and good men do not become soldiers'. Confucianism also complemented well the 'let barbarians fight barbarians' policy as it outsourced the grimy work of killing, leaving Chinese free to ponder the path of ethical gentlemen. The strategy had been effective but also demanded active Han involvement on the battlefield to achieve its finest results, such as when a combined Han-Wusun force defeated a Xiongnu army circa 71 BC. The approach promised tremendous short-term gains but overdependence on it later spelled trouble.

Political structures also weakened Han military capacity. With localities strengthening and local power bases growing assertive, the Eastern Han lacked centralized force. Once-well-functioning societal systems languished or vanished altogether, including conscription. Since the days of the Qin, the drafting of soldiers promoted a shared identity and, of course, supplied manpower for massive campaigns, which in turn became empire-wide enterprises exerting their own gravity upon a common identity.

Far from the expeditionary campaigns under the auspices of the 'Martial Emperor' Wu, China's posture backslid to the defensive, and to the inert. Military action could seize territory but it was settlers that consolidated those victories by holding and working the acquired lands. Now settlers flooded out of frontier regions to the comforts and safety of the south, ignoring the government's cash inducements to remain, and erased hard-won gains. Such people likely noted that if the seat of the Han government could move from Chang'an to Luoyang, far from the frontier, why should they remain as pawns of an outmoded, toothless policy?

In some ways, Ban Chao's background both reflects and challenges the nature of Eastern Han society. Born in a region near Chang'an, the capital of the Western Han, he hailed from a literary family, his father Ban Biao being the first author and compiler of the history *Book of Han*. After Biao's death, the work was carried on by Ban Chao's twin brother, Ban Gu, as well as his sister, Ban Zhao. (As will be seen in Chapter XIV, Ban Gu played an important part at the close of the Han-Xiongnu War, but also suffered due to the figures with whom he was associated.)

While Ban Chao belonged to an illustrious pedigree, his origin in western China near the old seat of the Western Han, Chang'an, was fitting, for the zip of the prior dynasty coursed in his blood. Ultimately, he opted for a career with the sword rather than the ink brush. A scholarly, articulate lad, Ban approached his duties with great seriousness. While working as a government scribe copying documents, he complained to his colleagues:

> A man of stature has no greater aspiration and ambition than to try to emulate Fu Jiezi and Zhang Qian, who were enfeoffed for their meritorious services in the foreign lands. How could one copy scripts with a brush forever?[2]

These two figures were apt, suggesting two sides of Ban Chao: the ruthlessness of Fu Jiezi, who in 77 BC had assassinated the king of Loulan in the Western Territories for defying the Han emperor, and the diplomacy and pioneering of Zhang Qian. In the meantime, though, Ban made his way through the Han bureaucracy, becoming a librarian – and then being jailed for some offence which has not been recorded. Yet Ban could take comfort in a meeting he once had with a soothsayer who saw future ennoblement in the young man:

> Your chin bone has the shape of a swallow, and your neck has the form of a tiger. It implies you will soar high and can eat meat. It is the physiognomy of a marquis from ten thousand *li* away.[3]

Ban indeed travelled far, for decades crossing the Western Territories, stamping out Xiongnu influence wherever he found it.

A United – then Partitioned – Xiongnu

The reclaiming of the Hexi Corridor, as well as their involvement with Khotan and elsewhere to resist King Xian in the Tarim Basin, suggested a resurgent Xiongnu who found common cause in resisting the Han. Yet such unity struggled to survive the loss of a leader. At the death of Chanyu Huduershi in AD 46 it was not his brother Bi, who by long-held customs of fraternal succession ought to have taken the title, but rather Huduershi's son Punu who sought to rule the empire. Infuriated, Bi refused to validate his nephew as *chanyu* and rallied eight tribes to his banner, and thus became *chanyu* of a faction known as the Southern Xiongnu. As had erupted in 60 BC, it would be civil war again, between Southern and Northern Xiongnu.

Perhaps more critical to his standing and prospects than the inclusion of those eight tribes, Bi quickly brokered a deal with the Han for support. The Southern Xiongnu received money and other aid, though this time, unlike the faction led by Huhanye in the previous century, they were kept on a short leash.

Like it had Huhanye's brother Zhizhi, this left Punu in a precarious spot and he trod much the same path as that earlier doomed *chanyu*. He attempted to strike a marriage alliance with the Han but was rebuffed. Occupying territory far to the north, flanked by the Han-allied Wusun, he could not easily ameliorate his conditions. With divided forces and a Xiongnu faction bolstered by Han support, Punu had to turn to other areas to exploit and leverage: the Tarim Basin. As *chanyus* before him had learned, controlling the resources of that region could change the course of their fortunes. Drawing on levies from the Tarim Basin, the Northern Xiongnu launched a series of attacks on the Hexi Corridor in AD 58; by AD 75 Punu's actions, combined with the near absence of Han resistance, led to its recapture. The Xiongnu had not held this strategically vital strip of land since the defection of the Hunye king in 121 BC. Now, if the Han wished to possess that territory again, they must fight for it.

The Han Army Stirs After Decades

The flourishing trade with the west surely made the Xiongnu projection in the Tarim Basin and Hexi Corridor a matter of such worry that even the inward-facing Eastern Han could eventually no longer tolerate it. Geng Bing, a Han general, persuaded Emperor Ming (AD 27–75, reigned 57–75) to again go on the offensive. For the first time in decades, the Chinese would launch a strike on the Xiongnu.

Circa AD 72, Geng campaigned north but, as they had so many times before, the Xiongnu fled, denying contact to the Han army. The Xiongnu adopted a more guerilla-type posture and their use of proxy forces drawn from client states in the Western Territories further made them an elusive target. Yet despite the neutral result of Geng's campaign, it signalled to the Xiongnu – and to Chinese subjects – the Han's drive to restore its place in the region and claw back its former holdings. Another expeditionary action was readied in AD 73. This time Ban Chao, the librarian-turned-soldier, joined the campaign.

The Battle of Yiwu

This campaign would target Xiongnu situated near the Tarim Basin city of Yiwu, known also as Hami (as it is named in modern China's Xinjiang Uyghur Autonomous Region). The commander was Dou Gu, member of a powerful clan at the court. It appears that, despite his encounter with the law, Ban Chao received a high rank upon accompanying this army. An officer named Guo Xun, who appears later in Ban's story, also rode along.

Near Yiwu the Han forces clashed with the Xiongnu, the first significant encounter between these armies in decades. Details are scanty but Ban – despite this may well being his first true service in the field – distinguished himself, killing many and impressing Commander Dou. And for the Han this was truly a momentous event, as ever since Wang Mang deposed the dynasty in AD 9 China possessed virtually no control or even presence in the region. Now, sixty-four years of absence had been reversed.

Yiwu was a critical site for agriculture, famed for its abundance as one of the more fertile regions of the Tarim Basin. The Han army established a garrison and a farming colony which could sustain it. Notably, Chinese practice colonized subjugated areas in the Tarim Basin, while the Xiongnu contented themselves with extracting its wealth, levies and other resources mostly from afar. Living subject to one's overlords must have been trying under either empire, though with the Xiongnu as their masters, the kingdoms at least maintained a degree of autonomy, so long as they did not fall short when the time came to pay.

Securing Han Vassals

His performance in the Battle of Yiwu proved Ban's merit sufficiently for Dou Gu to detail him to an important diplomatic mission west. Ban would serve as the chief of its military element and head of security. For a man skilled at war and at letters, this proved an ideal role, as quickly became evident at the delegation's first call.

Ban Takes Loulan

Well situated for northern and southern communication, Loulan was where King Xian of Yarkand attempted to block Han traffic in response to his demotion by their court. If Ban failed to establish a beachhead here now, the Chinese would lose access to a critical source of wealth.

When Ban and the Chinese embassy arrived, though the Loulan king received them with all due honours and hospitality, something struck Ban as amiss – perhaps the Han delegation was not the only visitor. After investigating, he uncovered the concealed encampment of a Xiongnu emissary and his retinue of men outnumbering Ban's force by four to one. Undoubtedly, they had come to manipulate the Loulan king, through payoffs or threats of violence.

Ban did not discuss the matter with the ambassador. 'He is a common civilian officer,' Ban explained to his soldiers. 'If we tell him our plans, he will let them leak out.'[4] Stealing through the darkness, he and his men ringed the encampment, with drummers placed at the rear. Setting fire to the tents, the favourable wind spread the flames, sending sleepy, bewildered men out into the night, only to be met by a hail of crossbow bolts.

Thirty Xiongnu fell directly to Ban's soldiers, while another hundred died in the flames. Ban showed he could act with decision, and his stealth and ruthlessness enabled him to annihilate a force which vastly outnumbered his own. His talents also extended to the dramatic, if grisly, display; identifying the Xiongnu emissary, Ban Chao beheaded him and presented that trophy to the Loulan king. Any vacillation by the king about which power his city ought to make its submission to quickly ended.

Reclaiming Loulan held value beyond the reopening of Silk Road commerce to China's benefit. As the first state seized for the Han by the general Zhao Ponu in 108 BC, Ban Chao's action was talismanic of the Han's return to the region. And Ban was only just getting started. In Ban the Chinese could accomplish much at low cost, without committing a great number of troops to expensive and dangerous expeditions. Indeed, when offered more men to fill out his thin ranks, Ban declined, preferring his own team of thirty trusted men for the rest of his long-range mission across the Western Territories.

Moving on to Khotan

From Loulan Ban and his elite unit rode west for Khotan. As the recent victor over Yarkand, Khotan's King Guangde – who had gulled King Xian of Yarkand out into the open, only to seize and murder him – now resisted Han entreaties. A Xiongnu officer stood by as the king's counsellor, or perhaps as his minder. No doubt beguiled by Ban's modest retinue, and ingratiating himself to his Xiongnu audience, King Guangde treated Ban with condescension. The king's shaman or court magician suggested Ban's horse would make a fine sacrifice to their god, perhaps thereby suggesting this might smooth matters with the king. Ban agreed, telling the magician to come collect the animal outside.

A short time later, Ban came before Guangde and – in what was becoming a signature move since Loulan – presented the dripping head of the magician. The aghast king hastened to prove how sincere he had been all along in his fidelity to the Han, and promptly had the remaining Xiongnu in his court murdered. Ban made Khotan a base of operations for himself but did not linger there long.

Controlling Kashgar

Proceeding onward, circa AD 73 Ban next came to Kashgar, known by the Chinese as Shule. The kingdom's location at the western edge of the Tarim Basin indicates its importance as a major Silk Road entrepot. Traders from Bactria, Sogdiana, and far beyond made Kashgar their port of call to buy and sell goods. Its value not lost on the Xiongnu, when Ban reached there, he found that the kingdom of Kucha held the city. This was the same Kucha, the rich state of the northern Tarim Basin set at the feet of the Celestial Mountain range, who with Xiongnu support had earlier defied King Xian. Again aided by the Xiongnu, recently Kucha had set one of its nobles named Douti on the Kashgar throne.

Perhaps because he recognized being overmatched militarily, Ban opted to settle this matter by guile. He sent a lone soldier into the city demanding the surrender of the king, who naturally refused. Apparently compensating for lack of numbers with pure gumption, the soldier managed to snatch the king and spirit him out of Kashgar. Thereupon Ban appeared before the people of the city, portraying himself as their liberator from Kuchan intriguing. He installed on the throne Zhong, a man of the original Kashgar royal line. Zhong and others demanded Douti's death. Surprisingly, despite his penchant for beheadings Ban released the Kuchan tyrant. Perhaps by denying the demand, Ban asserted his ultimate power over even a king. Years later, to his cost, Zhong would forget the lesson.

Revolt Across the Tarim Basin

By securing Loulan, Khotan, and Kashgar, Ban isolated the Xiongnu. Cut off from their support, it seemed they could only drift back into their northern wastes where food and fighting men were in short supply. Except the Xiongnu had been operating in this region for centuries and had laid the groundwork for a surprise; they had only to wait for the right moment to propagate unrest in the Tarim Basin by stirring up their allies and compelling other states to rebel. The death of Emperor Ming in AD 75 provided their opportunity, capitalizing on the inevitable distraction of the Han succession process to trigger a multi-pronged campaign. The kingdoms of Karashar and Kucha, both firmly in the Xiongnu orbit, assassinated Chen Mu, the Han 'protector general' or governor of the region, as well as his staff. Among them was Guo Xun, Ban's comrade from the Battle of Yiwu.

Meanwhile, ratcheting the pressure on the Han, the Northern Xiongnu dispatched 20,000 soldiers to attack the Han military agricultural colony at Jushi while stirring its local inhabitants to rebellion until the city fell. The Han, perhaps besotted with Ban's triumphs using his tiny elite team, dispatched a mere 300 troops to respond; en route they encountered a horde of Xiongnu and were wiped out. In Kashgar, a Xiongnu force invested the city in a lengthy siege, though they could not seize it.

While Han forces managed to dislodge the Xiongnu from Jushi in AD 76, the vagaries of a change in leadership doomed the newfound momentum. The young Emperor Zhang (AD 58–88) took the throne in AD 75, and different advisors and interests became ascendant; Zhang showed little taste for war in the Western Territories. Chen Mu's position as protector-general remained unfilled with a new appointee. The Yiwu garrison, established in the wake of Ban's first battle, was decommissioned. And Ban, despite his tremendous successes subjugating kingdoms, received an order to end all current campaigning and summoning him to the capital.

Ban Chao's Choice

With a diffident new emperor in power, the renewed push into the Western Territories could sputter just as it gathered itself, the short-sighted Han bureaucrats squandering hard-won gains. Ban's struggles and glories in the region would blow away like so much sand in a desert wind. Such thoughts must have weighed on his mind as he rode east.

By the time he reached his headquarters at Khotan, Ban made his decision to disregard the order. As he had in Loulan, acting with audacity and savvy, he could once again emulate the daring of his childhood heroes like the explorer Zhang Qian, who had continued his diplomatic mission even after ten years as a captive of the Xiongnu.

The first order of business: Kashgar. With Xiongnu resurgent across the Tarim Basin and the Han sending a clear signal of withdrawal, Kashgar broke free of Chinese suzerainty. Since Ban had installed King Zhong, his own man, there, the people had rebelled, buoyed by a renewed alliance with Kucha and a tiny principality named Weitou. Ban returned and put the Kashgar rebels to the sword, restored Zhong to the throne, then rode on to attack Weitou, slaying 600 there. Massing 10,000 soldiers from his bases of support in the region, Ban assaulted the restive city of Gumo (known also as Aksu) in the northern stretch of the Tarim Basin, where another 600 fell to him.

Yet so long as his forces remained so modest, two primary Xiongnu strongholds, Kucha and Karashar, remained beyond Ban's grasp.

Building an Invasion Force

Ban faced an impasse. From a position of Han weakness only a short time ago, he now stood at the precipice of bringing the region to heel and establishing lasting control for China. Yet his small-scale, elite force lacked the strength for serious operations against the formidable Kucha and Karashar. So it was time to set down his sword and take up the writing brush, to draft a letter to the emperor:

> Your subject has observed in private that our former emperors had wanted to open the passages to the Western Regions. Hence they sent troops to attack the Xiongnu in the north. It was followed by groups of envoys heading west; Shanshan [Loulan] and Yutian [Khotan] quickly submitted. And, now Jumi, Shache [Yarkand], Shule [Kashgar], Yuezhi [Kushan], Wusun and Kangju are all predisposed to submit to the Han court, longing to join our forces against Qiuci [Kucha] to open the Han Passage to the west.[5]

Ban cannily added that his proposal would only lightly tap government coffers, noting the arability of the areas he now controlled – thus a Han force could be largely self-sufficient. Dismissing himself as a 'shabby knife forged from lead', nevertheless Ban expressed his longing to see the Western Territories once more under Han domination.

Ban's plea persuaded the emperor, who dispatched 1,000 men – released prisoners and others – to join him in AD 80. While welcome, this would not tip the scales for him. So he looked to the Wusun, located north of the Western Territories and, after receiving imperial permission, formed an alliance, garnering 10,000 men for his brewing campaign. In AD 84, the court apportioned an additional eight hundred men to Ban.

Also in AD 84, Yarkand, ever blowing in the winds between the two powers, revolted against Han overlordship and allied with Xiongnu-backed Kucha. Its king conspired with Zhong, the Kashgar king whom Ban had personally set on its throne a decade earlier after driving out the Kucha-Xiongnu usurpers. The puppet-king had begun dancing on his own strings and Ban would now take him back in his grasp. With his newly amassed forces Ban laid siege to a fortress in the Kashgar region where Zhong had taken refuge. For six months Ban attempted to winnow the defences but the stronghold was proof against his efforts. His troops also sustained attacks by a Xiongnu-Kangju relief force in an attempt to lift the siege.

Though a steadfast warrior, Ban would turn to whatever means achieved his ends, and diplomacy might solve the matter now. Recently the Kushans had formed an alliance with Kangju. The Kushan state was likely the descendants of the Yuezhi, the nomadic nation with whom Zhang Qian had originally travelled to enter an alliance, only to be spurned. Using the Kushans not for their military might but their affiliation with Kangju, Ban gave a lavish 'gift' to the Kushans. The bribe was sufficient for their king to persuade the Kangju king to call off further action against the Han. Once the harassing attacks by Kanju troops ended, Ban's freedom to focus exclusively on the siege led to the quick seizure of Kashgar. The puppet-king Zhong, however, wriggled out of his grip and escaped off in Kangju's custody. But Ban and Zhong would meet again soon, for one last time.

Three years after his escape, Zhong sent a message to his former overlord that he wished to surrender. As Ban rode toward the rendezvous point, Zhong plotted his vengeance against the man who had controlled him for so long. In secret the deposed king assembled a cavalry force to ambush Ban's riders.

The two men and their retinues met at a banquet to celebrate the newfound peace between them. Yet Ban had only pretended to be hoodwinked by Zhong's ruse. When it came time to toast one another, Ban shouted to his men lying in wait, and they attacked the now-flustered cavalrymen. Ban seized Zhong and ended their years-long relationship by striking off his head.

With Kashgar under Han control again, Silk Road traffic could resume and a key strategic base had been restored. But Yarkand and Kucha still held out against Han domination, and they were hard targets. Defeating them would take not only great numbers, but also cunning. Ban raised an army of 25,000 and attacked Yarkand, still under the control of Kucha. While this represented a huge force for Ban, it was soon dwarfed by the 50,000 soldiers fielded by Kucha to meet him. He would need to draw off some of the enemy's strength.

Guile was called for again. Ban released or allowed for the escape of prisoners who reported to the king of Kucha what seemed like vital intelligence: the Chinese had split their forces to east and west and gone into retreat. Falling for the ruse, the Kuchan king raced to cut off Ban in the west, while another wing of the Kuchan army went east. Meanwhile, Ban swiftly doubled back and attacked Yarkand. With Yarkand's allies out of reach, the day was his, Ban slaying 5,000 and accepting the kingdom's surrender. Kucha beat a hasty retreat, only to soon surrender.

With this string of victories, after so long entirely absent or in the shadow of the Xiongnu, the Han re-established domination of the Western Territories. For his actions Ban was made governor of the Western Territories in AD 91. He had achieved a great deal for the empire, often with little more than a small band of handpicked soldiers and his wits. Arguably, he had outshone his childhood hero Zhang Qian. Yet something rankled him, so much that even an old man felt called to action. Karashar still defied the Han yoke, and not only had it stymied Ban's efforts in the region, but it also had blood on its hands for the 75 AD killing of Chen Mu, the man who once held Ban's new title of governor, and that of Guo Xun, Ban's former comrade in arms.

A Final Mission

Now in a position to call in huge levies from Han vassals, in autumn of AD 94 Ban assembled a gigantic force of 70,000 to assault Karashar. Nestled deep in the rugged Celestial Mountains, with points of egress readily defended, it promised to be an arduous campaign.

On the approach of Ban's army the Karashar forces destroyed bridges over the Yulduz River, though Ban discovered suitable fording points and his men waded across. The Karashar king fled deeper into the mountains, seeking to elude Ban, but fell into the Han general's clutches. Ban executed him at the same spot where, nineteen years earlier, he had killed the governor, Chen Mu. The various enemy heads Ban collected he had couriered to the capital. Displayed outside the quarters used by envoys from foreign lands when

Ban Chao (AD 32–102): Wielder of Brush and Sword

paying homage to the Han, they gave a nasty warning against the pursuit of independence from the Chinese empire.

The Han at last filled the protector-general's position, vacated at Chen Mu's assassination, with Ban Chao. He oversaw China's continued exploration and expansion west. In AD 97 he ordered a delegation to contact the Parthian Empire in Persia. One of his men on this long-range expedition likely reached the Persian Gulf but turned back when, had he continued on, he almost certainly would have made contact with the eastern edge of the Roman Empire.

Ban spent more than three decades in the Western Territories. A veteran of many battles and hard riding, he now wanted only to enjoy the land he had fought for so long. He returned to Luoyang in AD 102, only to die a month later.

Chapter XIV

Dou Xian (d. AD 92): Final Cog in the Han War Machine

When Ban Chao fought in the 73 AD Battle of Yiwu, he served under Dou Gu, a member of a well-connected clan with a deep military tradition. An earlier relation, Dou Rong, a celebrated war hero for the Xin dynasty under Wang Mang, later became an Eastern Han general. Gradually, through its men via military action, and its women via strategic marriages and concubinages, the Dou clan gathered significant political influence.

With no Chinese sovereign yet to rival Emperor Wu in gravitas and scope, increasingly the Eastern Han court was riven by clan intriguing. This hampered united action against the Xiongnu; luckily for the Han, though, the enemy was so degraded that even a mediocre man could become the unlikely last champion of China's centuries-long fight against them.

The Saving Grace of Nepotism

From early in his life a shadow hung over Dou Xian. His father was executed in AD 70 for an unknown crime against the court, and Dou's fortunes might have suffered irreparably from this. Yet he had a decided advantage as the scion of a storied clan and the elder brother of Empress Zhangde and, in the tradition of Wei Qing and Li Guangli before him, through this relation he gained a posting as a palace guard. However, unlike those famed generals, he did not use his role to pursue excellence on the battlefield, but rather lorded his power over others and strongarmed them to his financial advantage. This abuse of his privileges provoked the fury of the emperor, yet, perhaps owing to his sister's status, Dou escaped severe punishment.

When the emperor died in AD 88, a young son succeeded him, and with this turn of events opportunity blossomed for the Dou clan. Dou Xian's sister, the empress dowager, now became the regent. Quickly he expanded his reach in the court.

Soon, though, Dou's propensity for crime again landed him in trouble – and also set in train a series of events which would bring the Han-Xiongnu

War to a close, if not an entirely definitive one. Conspiring against the judge who presided over his father's death sentence nearly twenty years earlier, Dou arranged for the murder of the judge's son, whose head was struck off; Dou then offered this as a sacrifice at his father's tomb. Once again, he avoided justice, though surely this brought scandal, and it would have been only the august station of his sister, the empress dowager, that preserved him. However, once his crimes affected her, the immunity he had enjoyed vanished.

Dou suspected a man of having an illicit intimate relationship with his sister. Such a scandal coming to light might well jeopardize the standing of the Dou clan in court, including his own, so he had the man assassinated. At this offence, his sister imprisoned him, his fate now dangling by a thread. He needed some means to restore his standing. Fortunately for him, the Xiongnu would provide that chance.

The Xiongnu in the First Century AD

After the fall of the Western Han dynasty, relations between the Han and Xiongnu ranged from friend to sworn enemy. After the break between Huhanye and his brother Zhizhi in the first Xiongnu civil war of 60–53 BC, Huhanye's Han-allied faction served as a buffer against their northern brethren. But they had another value, working as a sort of police force to apprehend fugitives from Han justice. In AD 1 a king from the Western Territories to whom the Han denied sanctuary instead found it in Xiongnu lands; when the Xiongnu reported this to the Han court, they were reprimanded and ordered to turn over the fugitive, demonstrating the level of control the Han exercised over these tamed nomads.

But that was before Wang Mang toppled the Western Han and founded the Xin dynasty. Mighty upheaval followed, and only two decades later, when the restored Han emperor Gengshi sent an envoy seeking the Xiongnu return to the marriage alliance system, the *chanyu* retorted that now the emperor should instead pay homage to him. The reunited Xiongnu did not last long though, as in AD 46 their second civil war erupted.

Unlike the conflict which broke out in 60 BC, which ran seven years, this sprawled across decades. They partitioned into two groups. The weaker Southern Xiongnu faction, menaced by the Northerners, cleaved to the Han borders and even drifted within, joining the populations of the northern provinces. The Northern Xiongnu, though the dominant steppe power, found themselves marginalized and surrounded, a wounded, weakened, yet still-dangerous wolf. Isolated in the northern wastes, they led a hard-scrabble life, and those nearby sniffed their vulnerability.

Other tribal peoples, particularly the Xianbei, began probing for weaknesses. The Xianbei were old enemies; after he seized the position of *chanyu* from his father, Modun had gone to war against the Donghu, causing that confederation to split into the Xianbei and Wuhuan groups. In the ensuing period the Xianbei often subsisted as vassals of the Xiongnu. Now, in some ways, they would earn their centuries-delayed vengeance, especially with their latest ally – in AD 49 the Han forged an alliance with them, bestowing sumptuous gifts and offering the Xianbei bounties for Xiongnu heads. The new Chinese vassals proved their worth by immediately attacking a Xiongnu tribe. Atop the other pressures on them, the Xianbei aggression further hemmed in the Northern Xiongnu, pushing them westward and making their dependence on their Tarim Basin vassals and allies more acute. The Han then worked to neutralize this base of support.

While the Xianbei posed a hazard, it was the Southern Xiongnu who, though like a fish whose pond is carefully sized so that it can only grow to a certain breadth, were a true cause for worry. Recognizing the looming danger if the Southerners could persuade the Han to strike at the Northerners jointly, the Northern *chanyu* attempted to broker peace with the Han. In AD 51 or 52 their envoys asked to revive the marriage alliance between them, but learning from their success stymying Chanyu Zhizhi, China did not wish to risk the Xiongnu coalescing again; stoking mutual enmity and division served Han purposes far better. This supported the Han strategy of isolation and starving Xiongnu of aid, picking away at their strength and encouraging constituent tribes to break their affiliation with the *chanyu*.

Ban Chao's reclaiming of the Western Territories applied a stranglehold to Xiongnu supply lines and its pool of fighters. The Northern Xiongnu could look to some Southern comrades though, for life as the tamed creatures of the Han did not satisfy all Southern Xiongnu warriors. Probably the Southern *chanyu* worked with the Han to silence grumbling before it blazed into rebellion. And the Chinese posted guard units to block the flow of nomads defecting north.

Pressure mounted relentlessly on the Northern Xiongnu. At an unknown date Punu, the Northern *chanyu*, died and his relation, Youliu, took over in a tenure short-lived and disastrous. At an AD 87 battle with the Xianbei, the unfortunate leader fell into the enemy's hands, then was slain and flayed, his skin now a trophy and symbol of Xiongnu humiliation. Following that gruesome turn, a large part of the Northern faction, possibly 58 tribes and more than 200,000 people, then surrendered to the Han, no doubt preferring their custody to those of the Xianbei.

At this dark time, as the Northern faction teetered on the precipice of destruction, a new *chanyu*, his name unknown to history, stepped forward. His was a brave and thankless task, for in their near-crippled state his people were ripe for a massive Han attack. In AD 89 the Southern Xiongnu recognized this. Seeking to crush the Northerners at last, their *chanyu* sought and received Han support for a campaign. As well as giving the Southern Xiongnu their chance at long last to vanquish their Northern brothers, this would afford Dou Xian the circumstances to perhaps escape a death sentence.

The Battle of the Altai Mountains

While sitting in prison, Dou joined a distinctive fraternity. Ban Chao, Li Guangli, Zhang Qian, and Li Guang – perhaps even Princess Jieyou, by dint of her birth – had all run afoul of the Han; this drove each of them to risk wild gambles that they might redeem themselves in the court's eyes. The infant emperor over whom Dou's sister served as regent was growing up and had little love for the Dou clan. Now came the time for a grand gesture, so Dou volunteered for army service.

His previous military record is unrecorded. Perhaps as a relation of the general Dou Gu who had commanded Ban Chao, he was schooled in strategy or seasoned from actual combat. Or perhaps he simply benefited from the strength of his family name or to his proximity to the throne through his sister. But seemingly overnight Dou transformed from a prisoner mulling his execution to a general of a major campaign.

Xian personally commanded 4,000 cavalry, while another Han officer led an additional 4,000 men, and a Southern Xiongnu king rode at the head of a tumen (10,000). An additional tumen of Southern Xiongnu, led by their *chanyu*, Tuntuhe (reigned AD 88–93), streamed in. Finally, riders of the Qiang, the warlike people from the mountainous terrain of Sichuan and the Tibetan region, and other tribal groups, numbering 8,000, massed with the others at the Altai Mountain range.

This combined force, numbering 30,000 and composed of a broad coalition, represents the 'using barbarians to fight barbarians' dictum stretched to an extreme state. Han soldiers made up a comparatively meagre portion of this army, with only 8,000 troops called up – quite a contrast to the 300,000 assembled for the would-be ambush at Mayi in 133 BC by order of Emperor Wu. Undoubtedly the Western Han could never have fielded so many far-flung people under a single banner. In later years of the Eastern Han, this reliance on foreigners caused havoc. But in this battle, it served the Chinese well.

The grand army set out in the autumn of AD 89, marching north in three columns. The details of this final encounter are sparse, but the outcome decisive. After a clash the Xiongnu broke, the Northern *chanyu* put to flight. The coalition pursued the broken enemy, slaying 13,000 before 81 tribes surrendered to the Han. The army also seized 1,000,000 head of livestock – a blow which would have caused many subsequent deaths atop the significant battle casualties, the last remnants of the Northern Xiongnu, a force which had once caused China to tremble, left to starve in the frozen mountains.

It seems fitting the final blow struck against the Xiongnu would be executed by a perhaps untested functionary rather than a battle-seasoned soldier. Dou Xian lacked the verve and energy of Ban Chao, the quick thinking of Li Guang, the prowess of Huo Qubing. But this hardly mattered, for it was not the individual brilliance of a military leader but the Han system which prevailed in the end, with Dou Xian but a cog in the war machine. At long last the Chinese had found a way to keep their enemy divided and then outsource the bulk of any required fighting; it was a shrunken, weaker Xiongnu they had defeated than any of those soldiers of the Western Han ever faced.

A Victory Carved in Stone?

After the battle, Dou achieved a sort of apotheosis for the Han by scaling a mountain and at its peak performing a *feng* sacrifice, as Huo Qubing had done on behalf of the empire in 121 BC. These wild lands were now hallowed as Chinese territory and 'All under Heaven' was fit for rule.

The general also accepted a ceremonial cauldron from the Southern *chanyu* to present to the court. On his return to China, Xian basked in the accolades, his position in court rivalled only by the emperor. He did not enjoy the fruits of his victory for long, however. The honours and wealth heaped on a triumphant Han general could be mesmerizing but the fall after some inexcusable failing was steep – and in Dou's case, fatal. He, the Dou clan, and his circle of courtiers grew ever more presumptuous, abusing their power until, like other Han generals before him, he exhausted imperial patience. In AD 92, the man who presided over the death blow to the Han's greatest enemy was ordered to take his own life.

But he did leave behind a marker of his conquest at the Altai Mountains. Ban Gu, co-author of the history *Book of Han* and the famed general Ban Chao's twin brother, had accompanied Dou on the campaign. In the wake of the Xiongnu defeat, Dou ordered Ban Gu to memorialize the victory. (And, suffering the same fate so many who rose high within Han society, his association with Dou earned him in an early death in prison.) Chiselled into stone, the inscription recounted the victory:

> These intrepid men finally avenged the age-old rancour fermenting since the time of Gaozu and Emperor Wen. Thus, they illuminated the grandeur of the divine spirits of the ancestors of Han. They brought peace and security ... and expanded the realms and territories of the Kingdom, manifesting the power and influence of Han throughout the foreign lands.[1]

The Xiongnu Ride Out of History

The shattered remains of the Northern Xiongnu quickly lost any residual cohesion. Some drifted to the Ili River Valley, where they likely lived as wretched vassals of the Wusun who controlled these lands. Others joined the previous mass of Xiongnu who had submitted to the Xianbei in AD 87, again probably enduring unenviable circumstances. The Northern Xiongnu, crushed but not extirpated, petered out, morphing, bands acting independently or merging with other groups, their traditions and lineages living on in what came to be other steppe peoples, such as the Turks and Mongols.

Befitting a conflict as complex and sometimes amorphous as the Han-Xiongnu War, it defies the assignment of a clear ending date. While the Northern *chanyu* escaped death or capture at the Battle of the Altai Mountains, only an abject flock accompanied him now, more a corps of bodyguards than a combat-effective army. The Northern Xiongnu surely knew they would never recover from this latest blow and their *chanyu* in 90 or 91 AD announced his desire to surrender to the Han, probably on terms his predecessors would find laughable.

Dou Xian had dispatched men, including Ban Gu, to gain assurances of the coming surrender. Yet before this delegation reached him, Dou either had a change of heart or received contrary orders from the court, and instead he commanded a unit of 8,000 cavalry to attack the Northern *chanyu*'s camp. This Han force split into two wings and from east and west swooped down on the unsuspecting Xiongnu, killing the bulk of the previous battle's survivors and scattering the rest. Again the *chanyu* escaped, though this time never to return, and with him into oblivion rode the fortunes of his people and their chance to ever again challenge Han dominance of what had for centuries been their empire.

Epilogue: Reared in Each Other's Shadows

The two societies of Xiongnu and Han, so radically distinct in goals and temperament, nevertheless came into their own together. Whether the Xiongnu formed in response to the Qin threat or this merely strengthened their union, starting with the *chanyu* Modun, the bold handling of the Chinese over decades, plotted a path that brought the Xiongnu people riches and would inspire future steppe peoples. Similarly, the Han found use in the Xiongnu as a bulwark of their own identity, the architects of empire articulating the need to weld disparate kingdoms in the face of enemy depredation.

They relied on one another but also failed to gain mutual understanding. For the Han this likely delayed their victory and for the Xiongnu ensured their destruction.

Causes of the Xiongnu Defeat

What brought about the ignominious end for the Xiongnu? How did the Han prevail? The Xiongnu fought essentially as guerillas, albeit on a massive scale. Their raids and use of terrain as a weapon inflicted tremendous pain but could not pose an existential threat to the whole of China, nor was it intended to. Rather, *chanyus* like Yizhixie and several others calculated that if they applied painful costs the Han would relent in their campaigns and gladly pay the nomads for their safety again. For reasons of resources and of culture, the Xiongnu could not pursue another mode of warfare. To their misfortune, they underestimated the Chinese resolve to see the war through. Perhaps few monarchs, after Li Guangli had failed to take Dayuan in 101 BC, would have pledged several hundred thousand more soldiers to him so that he could make another attempt. But Emperor Wu, because he possessed the will, and more importantly because China possessed the resources, did so.

The Xiongnu political structure and its fundamental instabilities could simply not compete with Han powers of organization, even when – or perhaps, especially when – the Han stood at its weakest. No matter the skill and ferocity of its fighting men, the Xiongnu could never rival the Han's far-reaching bureaucracy enabling it to turn farmers into soldiers from across its vast empire. When the Han achieved its long-held dream of 'fighting barbarians with barbarians' by forming alliances with the Wusun, Xianbei, and others, their already massive well of manpower not only increased but they also benefited from the specific expertise of those tribal steppe warriors who implicitly understood how best to carry war to their common foe.

This method used against the Xiongnu, though effective, grew too attractive to the Chinese. Soon the propensity to outsource their combat to tribal peoples who were only nominal allies would hasten the weakening of the Han, especially in its frontier regions, and ultimately hasten the doom of the dynasty.

The Han Shrinks from the Steppe

The Eastern Han never placed the same importance on controlling its borderland domains as did the Western Han, and settlers there did not fail to interpret this policy change and act accordingly. Despite handsome subsidies, over the course of the first century AD and even in the decades after the Xiongnu defeat, Chinese subjects continued to pull up stakes and flee the frontier to the south. By the late second century AD much of its borderlands, and even the area surrounding its once mighty capital of Chang'an, fell out of Chinese control and into the hands of tribal groups. The locus of power had shifted east, its centre of gravity housed at the capital Luoyang, and projecting power and retaining its hold on western lands proved a fantasy to all but the most ardent and addled traditionalists.

Similarly, Han soldiers and officers dispatched to the borderlands generally lacked the seasoning of long service there, as the bulk of soldiers charged with their protection came from non-Chinese peoples. Chinese soldiers stationed at the frontiers were often convicts. With a legal code which offered harsh treatment for a dizzying number of offences, prisoners could opt for service on the frontier instead. What had once been a mark of glorious, heroic service at the frontier, where legends like Wei Qing and Huo Qubing through their feats carved their names in the annals, was now a means of punishment.

The Han built a network of vassal tribes to fight and buffer them against the Northern Xiongnu but, once the threat they were to counter vanished, the system lost its purpose – and the tribes lost their raiding targets and the wealth and social standing which could be wrung from them. So they turned instead on their masters. In the wake of the Xiongnu defeat, the Xianbei stepped in to claim their former domain. Emboldened, their allegiance to the Han did not long outlive that move. As the Xiongnu had while nominally bound to the Chinese, the Xianbei raided Chinese territory and eventually became so nettlesome that a Han army met them in the field, only to be all but massacred by their former allies.

Downfall of the Han

The Xiongnu were interwoven from the first with Han history, and even in their absence left a significant mark. Perhaps especially, the changes wrought to Han society in order to combat the Xiongnu now turned against the Chinese. The reliance on tribal soldiers also curtailed both the quality and numbers of Han soldiers. And with poor imperial control of frontier troops, the longstanding fear harboured by Han emperors came to pass. Just as it had with that comparable empire, Rome, warlordism took root. Commanders of foreign tribesmen and Chinese criminals demanded personal allegiance, not a distant, effete, eastern court besotted with poetry and Confucian debate. Court eunuchs, so useful to Emperor Wu as he pursued expensive, unpopular war, in the ensuing centuries teemed and organized into unshakeable blocs, seizing more power and eating at the foundations of the imperium.

The seizure of power by the warlord Dong Zhuo (d. AD 192) showed just how weak the court had become. As a young officer, Dong cut his teeth in the former Xiongnu territories and also stamped out rebellions by the restive Qiang tribes of the Tibetan Plateau. With his battlefield success came the unswerving loyalty of his soldiers. Fearful of his hold on this private army, several times the Han court summoned him to report to Luoyang but each time he refused. When he did appear at the capital it was at the head of his army to depose the emperor and install his own puppet on the throne. He later marched to Chang'an and occupied the former capital, but on his departure from Luoyang he plundered the tombs of the former Han emperors. The sitting emperor effectively was his puppet, the dynasty no longer ruling, until one of his bodyguards assassinated Dong Zhuo.

In the wake of his death multiple factions vied for power, their war persisting more than two decades until culminating in the last emperor's abdication in AD 220. More than 300 years of fractious kingdoms rising and toppling followed until at last the Sui dynasty stood up in AD 581 and imposed stability. The Tang dynasty (AD 618 – 906) then ushered in a renaissance for Chinese culture. The Han served as its template, a North Star guiding the burgeoning state back to refinement and imperial ambitions – and its emperors hungrily eyed the lands once subjugated by their predecessors, dreaming of the day they might, like their Han ancestors, swell their territories and again dominate their raw, uncultured northern neighbours.

Notes

Prologue: A Misread Prophecy
1. Watson (c), p 79.
2. Sima Qian, '秦始皇本纪.' Translation by author. Chinese Text Project. Accessed 21 October 2022. https://ctext.org/shiji/qin-shi-huang-ben-ji/ens.

Chapter I: The Chanyu Modun (d. 174 BC): First Emperor of the Steppe
1. Sima Qian, '匈奴列傳.' Translation by author. Chinese Text Project. Accessed 21 October 2022. https://ctext.org/shiji/xiong-nu-lie-zhuan.
2. Yap (a), p 67.
3. Yap (a), p 68.
4. Sima Qian, '匈奴列傳.' Translation by author. Chinese Text Project. Accessed 23 October 2022. https://ctext.org/shiji/xiong-nu-lie-zhuan.

Chapter II: Liu Bang (256–195 BC): From Rebel to Emperor
1. Watson (a), p 150.
2. Watson (c), p 80.
3. 'Chapter I. The Annals of Emperor Kao-tsu' 前漢書, *The History of the Former Han Dynasty* (The Institute for Advanced Technology in the Humanities, 2003). Accessed 19 September 2021.
4. '高祖本纪.' Translation by author. Chinese Text Project. Accessed 24 October 2022. https://ctext.org/shiji/gao-zu-ben-ji/ens.
5. Watson (a), p 76.
6. Watson (b), p 138.
7. Sima Qian, '高祖本纪.' Translation by author. Chinese Text Project. Accessed 25 October 2022. https://ctext.org/shiji/gao-zu-ben-ji/ens.

Chapter III: Emperor Wu of Han (156–87 BC): The 'Martial Emperor'
1. Yap (b), p 295.
2. Watson (b), p 146.
3. Sawyer (a), p 57.
4. Yü, p 37.
5. Watson (a), p 301.
6. Yap (a), p 107.
7. Watson (b), p 143.
8. Sima Qian, '匈奴列傳.' Translation by author. Chinese Text Project. Accessed 23 October 2022. https://ctext.org/shiji/xiong-nu-lie-zhuan.

9. Watson (b), p 145.
10. Sima Qian. '匈奴列傳.' Translation by author. Chinese Text Project. Accessed 29 October 2022. https://ctext.org/shiji/xiong-nu-lie-zhuan.
11. Sima Qian, '韩长孺列传.' Translation by author. Chinese Text Project. Accessed 1 November 2022. https://ctext.org/shiji/han-chang-ru-lie-zhuan/ens.
12. Watson (b), p 202.
13. Sima Qian. '平津侯主父列傳.' Translation by author. Chinese Text Project. Accessed 31 October 2022. https://ctext.org/shiji/ping-jin-hou-zhu-fu-lie-zhuan.
14. Watson (b), p 112.
15. Yap (a), p 150.
16. Yap (a), p 151.
17. Sima Qian, '韩长孺列传.' Translation by author. Chinese Text Project. Accessed 1 November 2022. https://ctext.org/shiji/han-chang-ru-lie-zhuan/ens.
18. Sima Qian, '韩长孺列传.' Translation by author. Chinese Text Project. Accessed 4 November 2022. https://ctext.org/shiji/han-chang-ru-lie-zhuan/ens.
19. Watson (b), p 114.

Chapter IV: Li Guang (d. 119 BC): The Bold and Blundering Bowman
1. Watson (b), p 128.
2. Watson (b), p 117.
3. Sima Qian, '李將軍列傳.' Translation by author. Chinese Text Project. Accessed 31 October 2022. https://ctext.org/shiji/li-jiang-jun-lie-zhuan.
4. Sima Qian, '李將軍列傳.' Translation by author. Chinese Text Project. Accessed 31 October 2022. https://ctext.org/shiji/li-jiang-jun-lie-zhuan.
5. A.C. Muller, 'The Analects of Confucius 論語 Translated by A. Charles Muller.' Resources for East Asian Language and Thought, 2021. http://www.acmuller.net/con-dao/analects.html.
6. Peers (a), p 74.
7. Sima Qian, '李將軍列傳.' Translation by author. Chinese Text Project. Accessed 5 November 2022. https://ctext.org/shiji/li-jiang-jun-lie-zhuan.
8. 'The Annals of Emperor Hsiao-wu.' 前漢書, *The History of the Former Han Dynasty* (The Institute for Advanced Technology in the Humanities, 2003). Accessed 17 September 2021. http://www2.iath.virginia.edu/saxon/servlet/SaxonServlet?source=xwomen/texts/hanshu.xml&style=xwomen/xsl/dynaxml.xsl&chunk.id=d2.24&toc.depth=1&toc.id=0&doc.lang=english
9. Sima Qian, '李將軍列傳.' Translation by author. Chinese Text Project. Accessed 31 October 2022. https://ctext.org/shiji/li-jiang-jun-lie-zhuan.
10. Watson (b), p 124.
11. Watson (b), p 124.
12. Sima Qian, '李將軍列傳.' Translation by author. Chinese Text Project. Accessed 31 October 2022. https://ctext.org/shiji/li-jiang-jun-lie-zhuan.

13. Watson (b), p 126.
14. Watson (b), p 126.
15. Sima Qian, '李將軍列傳.' Translation by author. Chinese Text Project. Accessed 31 October 2022. https://ctext.org/shiji/li-jiang-jun-lie-zhuan.

Chapter V: The Chanyu Yizhixie (d. 114 BC): Leader of an Embattled Empire

1. Sima Qian, '匈奴列傳.' Translation by author. Chinese Text Project. Accessed 4 November October 2022. https://ctext.org/shiji/xiong-nu-lie-zhuan.
2. Sima Qian, '匈奴列傳.' Translation by author. Chinese Text Project. Accessed 5 November 2022. https://ctext.org/shiji/xiong-nu-lie-zhuan.
3. Yap (a), p 187.

Chapter VI: Wei Qing (d. 105 BC): Strategist of the Battlefield and Court

1. Sima Qian, '衛將軍驃騎列傳.' Translation by author. Chinese Text Project. Accessed 1 November 2022. https://ctext.org/shiji/wei-jiang-jun-piao-qi-lie-zhuan.
2. Watson (b), p 166.
3. Watson (b), p 167.
4. Sima Qian, '衛將軍驃騎列傳.' Translation by author. Chinese Text Project. Accessed 6 November 2022. https://ctext.org/shiji/wei-jiang-jun-piao-qi-lie-zhuan.

Chapter VII: Huo Qubing (140–117 BC): Horseman with the Strength of the Steppe

1. Sima Qian, '衛將軍驃騎列傳.' Translation by author. Chinese Text Project. Accessed 3 November 2022. https://ctext.org/shiji/wei-jiang-jun-piao-qi-lie-zhuan.
2. Sima Qian, '衛將軍驃騎列傳.' Translation by author. Chinese Text Project. Accessed 3 November 2022. https://ctext.org/shiji/wei-jiang-jun-piao-qi-lie-zhuan.
3. Sima Qian, '衛將軍驃騎列傳.' Translation by author. Chinese Text Project. Accessed 5 November 2022. https://ctext.org/shiji/wei-jiang-jun-piao-qi-lie-zhuan.
4. Watson (b), p 171. The identity of the 'golden man' idol is unclear. It is possible, though unlikely, this was an image of the Buddha.
5. Sima Qian, '衛將軍驃騎列傳.' Translation by author. Chinese Text Project. Accessed 5 November 2022. https://ctext.org/shiji/wei-jiang-jun-piao-qi-lie-zhuan.
6. Watson (b), p 176.
7. Watson (b), p 178.

Chapter VIII: Zhang Qian (died c. 114 BC): Pioneer of the Silk Road

1. Sima Qian, '大宛列傳.' Translation by author. Chinese Text Project. Accessed 9 November 2022. https://ctext.org/shiji/da-wan-lie-zhuan.

2. Sima Qian, '大宛列傳.' Translation by author. Chinese Text Project. Accessed 9 November 2022. https://ctext.org/shiji/da-wan-lie-zhuan.
3. Hirth, p 94
4. Hirth, p 95
5. Hirth, p 95.
6. Hirth, p 95.
7. Hirth, p 94.
8. Sima Qian, '衛將軍驃騎列傳.' Translation by author. Chinese Text Project. Accessed 10 November 2022. https://ctext.org/shiji/wei-jiang-jun-piao-qi-lie-zhuan.
9. Hirth, p 101.
10. Hirth, p 101.
11. Hirth, p 101.
12. Hirth, p 103.

Chapter IX: Princess Jieyou (d. 49 BC): Peace Bride and Han Operative
1. Sima Qian, '大宛列傳.' Translation by author. Chinese Text Project. Accessed 17 November 2022. https://ctext.org/shiji/da-wan-lie-zhuan.
2. Hirth, pp 100–1.
3. Hulsewé, p 148.
4. Hulsewé, p 144.
5. Ban Zhao, '女誡.' Translation by author. 维基文库. Accessed 19 November 2022. https://zh.m.wikisource.org/zh-hant/%E5%A5%B3%E8%AA%A1.
6. Hulsewé, p 148.
7. Yap (a), p 219.
8. Hulsewé, p 150.
9. Hulsewé, p 150–1.
10. Hulsewé, p 154.
11. Hulsewé, p 158.

Chapter X: Li Guangli (d. 88 BC): Hunter of Heavenly Horses
1. Watson (b), p 240.
2. Sima Qian, '大宛列傳.' Translation by author. Chinese Text Project. Accessed 13 November 2022. https://ctext.org/shiji/da-wan-lie-zhuan.
3. Sima Qian, '大宛列傳.' Translation by author. Chinese Text Project. Accessed 13 November 2022. https://ctext.org/shiji/da-wan-lie-zhuan.
4. Watson (b), p 246.
5. Sima Qian, '大宛列傳.' Translation by author. Chinese Text Project. Accessed 13 November 2022. https://ctext.org/shiji/da-wan-lie-zhuan.
6. Sima Qian, '大宛列傳.' Translation by author. Chinese Text Project. Accessed 13 November 2022. https://ctext.org/shiji/da-wan-lie-zhuan.
7. Watson (b), p 249.
8. Watson (a), Epigraph.
9. Yap (a), p 265.
10. Yap (a), p 265.

Chapter XI: The Chanyus Zhizhi (d. 36 BC) and Huhanye (d. 31 BC): A Broken Brotherhood
1. Watson (b), p 244.
2. Barfield, pp 61–2.
3. Yap (a), pp 354–5.
4. Yap (a), p 355.
5. Yap (a), p 374.
6. Yap (a), p 375.
7. Yap (a), p 377.
8. Yap (a), p 394.

Chapter XII: King Xian of Yarkand (d. circa AD 62): Han Ally Gone Rogue
1. Barfield, p 70.
2. Hill (a), p 37.
3. Hill (a), p 41.
4. Hill (a), p 41.

Chapter XIII: Ban Chao (AD 32–103): Wielder of Brush and Sword
1 Grousset, p 42.
2. Yap (b), p 526.
3. Yap (b), p 527.
4. Grousset, p 42.
5. Yap (b), p 533.

Chapter XIV: Dou Xian (d. AD 92): Final Cog in the Han War Machine
1. Yap (b), p 516.

Bibliography

Atwood, C.P., *Encyclopedia of Mongolia and the Mongol Empire* (New York: Facts on File, 2004).
Baldick, J., *Animal and Shaman: Ancient Religions of Central Asia* (New York: New York University Press, 2004).
Ban Zhao, 维基文库. '女誡.' https://zh.m.wikisource.org/zh-hant/%E5%A5%B3%E8%AA%A1.
Barfield, T.J., *The Perilous Frontier: Nomadic Empires and China* (Cambridge, MA: Basil Blackwell Inc, 1989).
Beckwith, C.I., *Empires of the Silk Road: A History of Central Eurasia from the Bronze Age to the Present* (Princeton, NJ: Princeton University Press, 2009).
Chinese Text Project. '史記 - Shiji.' https://ctext.org/shiji.
Di Cosimo, N., *Ancient China and Its Enemies: The Rise of Nomadic Power in East Asian History* (New York: Cambridge University Press, 2002).
Grousset, R., (N. Walford, trans). *Empire of the Steppes: A History of Central Asia* (Rutgers, NJ: Rutgers, The State University of New Jersey, 1970).
Hill, J.E. (a), *Through the Jade Gate – China to Rome: A Study of the Silk Routes 1st to 2nd Centuries CE, Volume I* (2015).
Hill, J.E. (b), *Through the Jade Gate – China to Rome: A Study of the Silk Routes 1st to 2nd Centuries CE, Volume II* (2015).
Hulsewé, A.F.P., *China in Central Asia – The Early Stage: An Annotated Translation of Chapters 61 and 96 of the History of the Former Han Dynasty* (Leiden: E.J. Brill, 1979).
Karasulas, A., *Mounted Archers of the Steppe 600 BC – AD 1300* (Oxford: Osprey Publishing, 2004).
Lattimore, O, *Inner Asian Frontiers of China* (New York: American Geographical Society of New York, 1951).
Lewis, M.E., *The Early Chinese Empires: Qin and Han* (Cambridge, MA: Harvard University Press, 2007).
Loewe, M., *Everyday Life in Early Imperial China* (Indianapolis, IN: Hackett Publishing Company Inc, 2005).
Loewe, M., *Faith, Myth and Reason in Han China* (Indianapolis, IN: Hackett Publishing Company Inc, 2005).
Lynn, J.A., *Battle* (Boulder, CO: Westview Press, 2003).
Mayor, A., *The Amazons: Lives & Legends of Warrior Women Across the Ancient World* (Princeton, NJ: Princeton University Press, 2014).

Muller, A.C., 'The Analects of Confucius 論語 Translated by A. Charles Muller', Resources for East Asian Language and Thought. http://www.acmuller.net/con-dao/analects.html.

Ostler, N.O., *Empires of the Word: A Language History of the World* (New York: Harper Collins Publishers, 2005).

Peers, C.J. (a), *Soldiers of the Dragon: Chinese Armies 1500 BC – AD 1840* (Oxford: Osprey Publishing, 2006).

Peers, C. (b), *Battles of Ancient China* (Barnsley, South Yorkshire: Pen & Sword Military, 2013).

Sawyer, R. (a), *The Seven Military Classics of Ancient China* (Boulder, CO: Westview Press, Inc, 1993).

Sawyer, R. (b), *Ancient Chinese Warfare* (New York: Basic Books, 2011).

Sinor, D. (ed), *The Cambridge History of Early Inner Asia* (Cambridge: Cambridge University Press, 1990).

'The History of the Former Han Dynasty', (University of Virginia: The Institute for Advanced Technology in the Humanities, 2003). http://www2.iath.virginia.edu/saxon/servlet/SaxonServlet?source=xwomen/texts/hanshu.xml&style=xwomen/xsl/dynaxml.xsl&chunk.id=tpage&doc.view=tocc&doc.lang=bilingual

Waldron, A, *The Great Wall of China: From History to Myth* (Cambridge: Cambridge University Press, 1990).

Watson, B. (a), *Records of the Grand Historian: Han I* (Hong Kong: Columbia University Press, 1993).

Watson, B. (b), *Records of the Grand Historian: Han II* (Hong Kong: Columbia University Press, 1993).

Watson, B. (c), *Records of the Grand Historian: Qin* (Hong Kong: The Research Centre for Translation, The Chinese University of Hong Kong, and Columbia University Press, 1993).

Yap, J.P. (a), *Wars with the Xiongnu: A Translation from Zizhi Tongjian* (Bloomington: AuthorHouse, 2009).

Yap, J.P. (b), *Western Regions: Xiongnu and Han* (2019).

Yü, Ying-shih, *Trade and Expansion in Han China: A Study in the Structure of Sino-Barbarian Economic Relations* (Berkeley and Los Angeles: University of California Press, 1967).

Index

Archery,
  Chinese, 41
  crossbows, 41, 44
  Xiongnu, 44

Ban Chao, 133–43
  capturing key cities of Tarim Basin, 137–8
  alliance with Wusun, 141
  alliance with Kushan, 141
  dispatching delegation to Parthia, 142
Ban Gu, 134, 148–9
Ban Zhao, 95
Battle of Altai Mountains, 146–7
  see also Dou Xian
Battle of Baideng, 18–20
Battle of Mobei, 50–1, 63–4, 71–2
Battle of Yiwu, 136
Book of Changes, 30, 101
Book of Han, 19, 95, 134, 148
Border of Han and Xiongnu lands, 22
  contact between Chinese and Xiongnu, 17–18
  see also Great Wall

Chang'an, 16, 27, 93, 118, 122, 126, 151, 152
Chanyu Huduershi, 127–8
Chanyu Huhanye, 116–17
  submission to Han, 117–18, 122
Chanyu Junchen, 52, 53
Chanyu Laoshang, 26, 84
Chanyu Luanti Touman, 3, 6
Chanyu Modun,
  escape from Yuezhi captivity, 7
  assassination of father, 8–9
  struggles with the Donghu, 11
  struggles with the Yuezhi, 12
  letter to Han empress dowager, 21
  death, 26
  see also Military of the Xiongnu Empire, Governance of the Xiongnu Empire, Marriage alliance
Chanyu Punu, 135
Chanyu Yizhixie, 52–64
  power struggle with nephew Yudan, 53–4
  as battlefield commander, 61–2
  escape from the Battle of Mobei, 72

  see also Battle of Mobei, Governance of the Xiongnu, Huo Qubing
Chanyu Zhizhi, 116–17
  alliance with Kangju, 119–120
  Battle of Zhizhi, 120–2
Chariots, 6, 18, 19, 27, 41, 44, 65, 71–2, 77
Chu-Han Contention, see Liu Bang
Civil Wars of the Xiongnu Empire
  60–53 BC, 116–18
  beginning AD 46, 145
  partition of Xiongnu into Northern and Southern factions, 135, 145–7
Confucianism, 13, 25, 125, 127
Conscription of Chinese soldiers, 42
  by the Qin, xiii
  by the Han, 18, 103, 134

Dayuan, 87–8, 101–108, 115, 131
Dong Zhuo, 152
Dou Xian, 144–5, 147–9

Eastern Han dynasty, 126–7
  clan intriguing, 144
  Luoyang as capital city, 126–7, 152
  military culture, 133–4
  retreating from steppe, 151
  see also Ban Chao, Dou Xian, King Xian of Yarkand
Emperor Gaozu, see Liu Bang
Emperor Jing of Han, 25
Emperor Wen of Han, 21–2, 40
Emperor Wu of Han, 21–35
  cult of personality, 30
  quest for immortality, 30
  reliance on occult, 30
  death, 112–13
  see also Heavenly Horses, Huo Qubing, Li Guang, Li Guangli, Mayi, Wei Qing

Feng and shan sacrifices, 79, 148
Feudalism, 18, 32
Ferghana Valley, 87
Five Baits, 22
Four Seas and Eight Wastes, 83

Ganfu, 85–7
Gongsun Ao, 65

Governance of the Xiongnu Empire,
  role of chanyu, 6
  political structure, 9–10, 150–1
  leadership challenges, 54
  autumn assemblies, 54–5, 63
  succession, 116
  see also Civil wars of the Xiongnu Empire, Marriage alliance
Great Wall, xiii–xiv, 20, 22–3, 32, 43

Han dynasty (Western), 17
  bureaucracy in, 14, 51, 66–8, 150–1
  rebellions against, 17, 24
  fall of Western Han dynasty, 125
  clan influence, 125
  see also Eastern Han dynasty, Liu Bang, Military of the Han dynasty, Rebellion of the Seven States
Han Xin, 17–18
Hexi Corridor, 26, 45, 76, 93, 128
  Xiongnu loss of, 62–3
  Xiongnu recapture of, 135
  see also Huo Qubing
Heavenly Horses, 87, 101
  see also Li Guangli
Horses and horsemanship,
  Xiongnu, 5–6, 57–8
  Han demand for horses, 18, 71, 95
  Chinese, 77–8
  see also Heavenly Horses, King Wuling of Zhao
Hunye king, 62–3, 76
Huo Qubing, 62, 71, 73–80
  in 123 BC campaign, 74
  in 121 BC campaigns, 75–6, 78–9
  performing *feng* and *shan* sacrifices, 79
  tomb of, 80
  see also Chanyu Yizhixie, Hexi Corridor, Hunye king, Wei Qing

Inscription of Yanran, 148–9

Jade Gate, 85, 130

Kangju, 119–20, 141
Karashar, 139, 140, 142–3
Kashgar, 138, 140
Khotan, 131–2, 138
King Wuling of Zhao, 77
King Xian of Yarkand, 129–32
Kucha, 129, 130–1, 138–42
Kushan, 141

Lady Feng, 99
Legalism, xii, 13, 127
Li Gan, 51, 72, 73

Li Guang, 39–51, 71
  in Rebellion of the Seven States, 40
  early ruse against the Xiongnu, 45
  in 129 BC campaign against Xiongnu, 45–6
  suicide, 51, 72
  see also Archery, Battle of Mobei, Li Gan, Wei Qing, Zhang Qian
Li Guangli, 103–12
  campaigns against Dayuan, 103–108
  campaigns against Xiongnu, 108–12
  see also Emperor Wu of Han, Occult
Li Ling, 109–10
Li Mu, 33
Literacy in China, 42, 63, 67
Liu Bang, 13–20
  ascension to throne, 16
  death, 20
  leadership style, 16
  victory in Chu-Han Contention, 14–16
Liu Xijun, 95–6
Loulan, 129–30, 137

Mandate of Heaven, 16
Marriage alliance, 20, 21–5, 52
  benefits to Xiongnu, 23, 25–6, 55–6
  Han debate over 135 BC renewal, 30–2
  see also Chanyu Yizhixie, Liu Xijun, Princess Jieyou, Wusun people, Zhang Qian
Mayi, 17
  Battle of, 33–5, 52
  Han debate over, 30–2
Meng Tian, xiii–xiv
Military of the Han dynasty,
  arms and armour, 44
  campaigns against Xiongnu,
    129 BC, 45–6
    123 BC, 48
    121/120 BC, 48
    AD 72, 136
  command, 66–7
  doctrine, 18
  order of battle, 43
  Qin influence upon, 18
  strategy against the Xiongnu, 83, 146
Military of the Xiongnu Empire,
  campaigns against the Han,
    in 166 BC, 27–28, 40
    in 125 BC, 61–2
  doctrine, 57–8
  raids, 23–4, 59
  soldiers, 56–9
  tactics, 58–9
  use of terrain, 61
  weaponry, 60
  see also Chanyu Modun, Chanyu Yizhixie

Occult, 30, 49–50, 111
    see also Book of Changes, Emperor Wu of
        Han, Li Guangli
Ordos Plateau, xii
    Xiongnu expulsion from, xiii, 3, 6–7
    Xiongnu recapture of, 12
    Han recapture of, 68

Princess Jieyou, 97–100

Qiang people, 63, 152
Qin dynasty, xii–xiv
    invasion of the Ordos Plateau, xiii–xiv
    rebellion against and fall of, xiv, 14
    standardization of writing, 42, 68
    victory over the Warring States, 42
    see also Conscription of Chinese soldiers,
        Legalism, Shi Huangdi

Rebellion of the Seven States, 28–9, 40
    see also Li Guang
Records of the Grand Historian, see Sima Qian

Shi Huangdi, xii
    death, xiv, 13
    mausoleum of, 13
Silk Road, 89–90, 93, 128, 129, 138, 142
    see also Ban Chao, King Xian of Yarkand,
        Tarim Basin, Western Territories,
        Zhang Qian
Sima Qian, xii, 6, 110
Spring and Autumn Period, 42
Strategic manuals, 22, 42, 74–5
    see also Sun Tzu, Warring States period
Su Jian, 68, 70
Sun Tzu, 66–7

Tengri, see Xiongnu Empire religion
Tianxia, xi, 83
Tarim Basin,
    imperial designs on by Han and
        Xiongnu, 128
    kingdoms of, 62
    revolt against Han, 139–42
    Xiongnu suzerainty over, 25, 62
    see also Ban Chao, King Xian of Yarkand,
        Li Guangli, Western Territories,
        Chanyu Zhizhi
Trans-Oxiana (Sogdiana), 88

Wang Hui, see Mayi
Wang Mang Interregnum, 125–6
Wang Zhaojun, 122
Warring States period, xii, 17, 22, 41, 42, 66
    see also Qin dynasty

Wei Qing, 51, 52, 61, 65–72
    campaigns in,
        129 BC, 65–66
        127 BC, 68
        124 BC, 69
    promotion to supreme commander, 69
    prophecy of greatness, 65
    see also Battle of Mobei, Chanyu Yizhixie,
        Huo Qubing, Li Guang, Zhang Qian,
        Zhao Xin
Wen and wu, 25
Western Territories, 105, 114–15,
    118–19, 128
    loss by Xin dynasty, 126
    assassination of Protector General Chen
        Mu, 139
    see also Ban Chao, King Xian of Yarkand
Wuhuan people, 115
Wusun people, 91–3, 94–100
    conflict with the Xiongnu, 25
    interaction with Zhang Qian, 91–3
    Han alliance with, 92–3, 94, 101, 141
    campaigns with Han against Xiongnu,
        98, 115–16

Xianbei people, 146, 149, 151–2
Xianyang, xiii
Xiongnu Empire,
    meaning of name, 3
    origins, 4
    languages spoken, 4
    religion, 4–5
    strategy against the Han, 54–6, 150
    see also Civil wars of the Xiongnu Empire,
        Governance of the Xiongnu Empire,
        Marriage alliance, Military of the
        Xiongnu Empire

Yarkand, 128–9, 141, 142
Yin and yang, xiii
Yuezhi people, 7, 12, 25–6, 31, 141
    Zhang Qian's mission to, 84, 88–9

Zhang Qian, 48–9, 52, 83–93
    captivity among the Xiongnu, 85–6, 89
    mission to the Yuezhi, 84–90
    military service in 129 BC, 90
    mission to the Wusun, 91–3
Zhao Xin, 61–2, 64, 66, 70
Zhonghang Yue, 26–7
Zhou dynasty, 41, 42

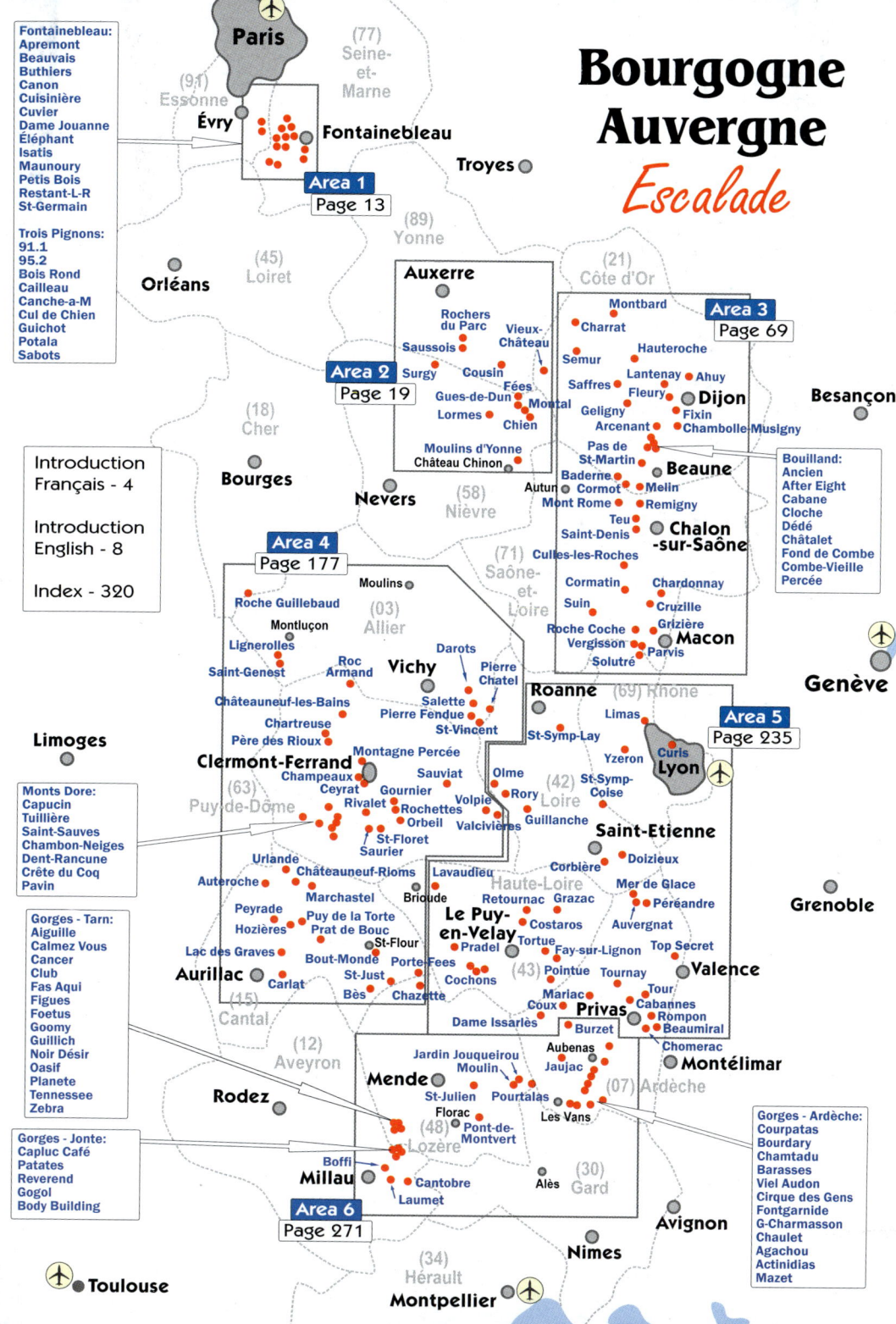

Bourgogne Auvergne Escalade
by David Atchison-Jones (Author, illustrator, photographer & graphic designer)

Jingo Wobbly – Bilingual Topo Guides - France Roc-1
First Published in June 2021
By Jingo Wobbly Publishing (www.jingowobbly.com)
(An imprint of Vision PC).
Holmwood House, 52 Roxborough Park,
Harrow-on-the-Hill, London. HA1 3AY   Great Britain

Copyright © David Atchison-Jones 2021

All rights reserved. No part of this publication may be reproduced, stored in a retrieval system, or transmitted in any form or by any means, electronic, mechanical, photocopying, recording or otherwise, without prior written permission of the copyright owner, and especially not to be copied or published online.

A CIP catalogue record is available from the British Library - printed in Roma, Italy.

ISBN   978-1-873 665-17-6   (FRANCE ROC 1)

This book by definition is a climbing guidebook, and not a climbing safety book, and has no instructions or directions with regard to any safety aspect of climbing or general safety in climbing areas. Please seek professional safety advice before ever entering any climbing environment.

A climbing guidebook, is a collection of past climbing knowledge from a variety of sources. It cannot be regarded as either fact or fiction, since the information has been generally handed down across the generations, and is always open to the interpretation of the reader. We do of course however, make every effort to ensure that the information included in the guidebook is as up to date, and as accurate as possible at the time of going to press, but we unfortunately cannot guarantee any complete accuracy. Any information included within the sponsor advertisements are the sole responsibility of the advertiser. The publisher and editor cannot accept responsibility for any consequences arising from the use of this book, and do not accept any liability whatsoever for injury or damage caused by anyone arising from the use of this book.

The inclusion of any boulder or cliff in this guide, does not mean that anybody has any right of access whatsoever. All climbers and visitors should be aware that there may be strict access and conservation issues at any of the areas included in this guide, and should read and understand all notices, before climbing.

If there is any information that you feel is improper, or that you feel could be updated, please write to us or email us (info@jingowobbly.com) at our publishing address, where we will gladly collect the information for future editions. Latest information can be found at **www.jingowobbly.com**

Special acknowledgements: Ouvreur, rééquipment & information: Daniel Taupin, Jacky Godoffe, Jo Montchausse, Oleg Sokolsky, Jean-Claude Droyer, JJ Naels, Sebastien Frigault, Bart van Raaij, Philippe Le Denmat, Loïc Le Denmat, Eric Letot, Jean-Yves & Stephanie Salin, Gilles Deschamps, René Hopf, Jean Baptiste Capicot, Luc,Alain, Philippe Martin, Eric Mutin, Luc Pillet, Hervé Delacour, Olivier Rollet, Romain Petit, Mathieu Midonet, Thomas Boisgard, Jean-Luc Deriaz, P. Courtois, P. Dahen, P. Delachambre, Jean Fontaine, Didier Pitelli, Thomas Brun, François Bonneviale, Eric Brunel, Eric Vassard, Jean Noël Pascal, Yannick Dupin, Pierrick Denier, Calmus Pascal, Eric Vales, Jean-Luc Scola, J-F Flageat, Alain Finet, Jean-Yves Gerbet, Jean Wiedmer, Philippe Gleizes, André Marceaux, Bobbou, François Bonnevialle, Le Boss, Pierre Duroché, Mickael Vallesi, Marc Burger, Jérôme Bernier, Raphael Kervella, François Carton, Michel Raquin, Jean-Baptiste Bardin, Aurélin Pais, Julien Méral, Benoit Heintz, David Vigouroux, Alexandro et Gabriella Ségara, Denis Collangettes, G. Monneron, M. Chalier, Sébastien Messager, Philippe Poitevin, Emie Blanc, Louis-Alexis Pittie, Tom Vaille, Maxime Boulot, Alfred Jassaud, Jean-Luc Brosson, Christian Fontugne, Robert Courbis, Jean Mathieu, Guilhem Trouillas, David Perrier, Emilien Lecomte, Flavien Guerimand, Abel Moulin, Christophe Bernard, Yvan Armand, Alexandre Dupont, Sébastien Augey, Philippe Cappeau, Sébastien Ranc, Ivan Sorro, Jean Pierre Coq, Olivier Obin, Raphael Storbecher, Charlotte Durif; and so many other people not mentioned.

Editorial: A giant thank you to everyone who has contributed to the making of this book over several years. A big thankyou to Virginie Percival and for the translations, and to Carrie for endless days of climbing, belaying and musical partying.

David Atchison-Jones

Front cover photo: **PACIFIC HIGHWAY GAUCHE 8a,** *Jean-Yves Salin [Bouilland, Côte d'Or]*
Title Page: **LES SEINS DE GLACE 6a,** *Carrie Atchison-Jones [Puy de la Tourte, Cantal]* ▷
Back cover photo: **ARC EN CIEL 6c,** *Gregory Lefaux [Cormot, Côte d'Or]*